Living
Inside Out

Living Inside Out

Learning How to Pray the Serenity Prayer

Jan G. Linn

Chalice Press
St. Louis, Missouri

Biblical quotations, unless otherwise noted, are from the *New Revised Standard Version Bible (with Apocrypha)*, copyright 1989, Division of Christian Education of the National Council of the Churches of Christ in the USA. Used by permission.

Those quotations marked RSV are from the *Revised Standard Version* of the Bible, copyrighted 1946, 1952, © 1971, 1973.

Cover illustration: Glenn Myers
Art Director: Michael Dominguez

10 9 8 7 6 5 4 3 2 1

Library of Congress Cataloging–in–Publication Data
Linn, Jan.
    Living inside out : learning how to pray the Serenity prayer / Jan G. Linn.
      p. cm.
    Includes bibliographical references.
    ISBN 0-8272-2123-1 (pbk.)
    1. Serenity prayer. 2. Spiritual life—Christianity. 3. Prayer groups—Christianity. I. Title.
BV284.S47L56 1994   94-12023
242'.4—dc20

Printed in the United States of America

To my Mother

for who she is and
has always been

Contents

Acknowledgments

This book has been in the making for a long time. The impetus for these thoughts on the Serenity Prayer was occasioned by an invitation several years ago from First Christian Church of Leavenworth, Kansas, to deliver a series of lectures whose focus would be personal renewal. I am grateful for the hospitality of that congregation, and its pastor, Bill Nowlan, and their positive response to the material.

In a curious way, however, after that series of lectures I felt the need to live with this material for a while in order to experience the transformative power of the Serenity Prayer in my own life at a deeper level. I needed to learn more about how to "pray" this prayer, and not simply say it, something the book explains in detail. As I did this, and as the result of many conversations with people struggling with very difficult personal situations, the truth of this simple little prayer became more evident. Its wisdom seemed to speak to any number of different circumstances that all people face. There is hardly a problem or personal struggle in life in which working the Serenity Prayer does not help.

Once I put the material into manuscript form I decided to use it in a class I teach on spiritual formation. I am indebted to those students in the class, and several not in the class, who read the manuscript and made suggestions that improved the practical application of the material significantly.

To my colleague, Loren Broadus, I want to express special appreciation for reading the material in its early manuscript stages and for providing several helpful suggestions. Once again, thanks also must go to my editor, David Polk, for his steadfast interest in the book, and for his wise discernment of the appropriate sequence for publishing the recent writings I have sent to him.

Finally, it is my hope that the reader will find in these pages a practical guide to learning how to live life in a new way, from the inside out. It is the truest way I know to a life of daily peace for which all of us long.

Jan G. Linn
Easter Week, 1994

Introduction

Psychiatrist Scott Peck begins his longtime popular book, *The Road Less Traveled*, with three simple words, "Life is difficult." That much most people know very well. But Peck goes on to say that the mere acknowledgment that life is not easy is itself transforming: "Once it is accepted, the fact that life is difficult no longer matters."[1] Peck believes that the fact that life is always difficult means living rather than merely existing requires us to face difficulties with the discipline to overcome them. In other words, *meaning-full* living is possible only when we take ultimate responsibility for the quality of our living. No one else can make us happy. No one else can give our lives meaning and purpose or a sense of fulfillment. All of that, Peck says, comes from within.

We shall have more to say later about the central role we play in our own happiness. At the same time, though,

1

the need to accept personal responsibility for ourselves in all circumstances should not lead us to minimize the harshness of the pain and struggle of trying to live meaningful lives. Life is not only difficult. Life is not only suffering.[2] Life is not only unfair. Many times life flies to pieces. Things do happen that devastate us, and when they do we can easily feel overwhelmed by the situation. In such moments it hardly ever helps to be told that we simply have to rise above circumstances. When life goes to pieces, the most urgent need of the moment is to know that we can survive. It may seem obvious to everyone else that one can survive the worst of circumstances. People have before. But to the person whose life is flying to pieces, survival doesn't feel so obvious, or even desirable. Only as the person recovers a sense of balance is one able to take responsibility for the quality of one's living.

There is no worse experience than feeling as if your life is flying to pieces. What is more, such a feeling is more common than many of us realize. We tend to think that a sense of desperation or the feeling that we cannot cope with the circumstances of our lives happens to someone else, but not to us. As one woman who came to talk to me said, "I don't get depressed." But she did. Such feelings come to all of us—to me and to you. Blue collar workers and company executives have them. Rich and poor, the wise and the foolish, the literate and the illiterate, the powerful and the powerless, the young and the old—all have them. No one is exempt from the possibility of facing circumstances that feel out of control, or from reaching a point in life when any meaning we once had in life seems to be gone.

The fact is, most of us are subject to a wide variety of mood swings that affect how we feel about life. Researchers have found that only 2 percent of people are in what can be considered a cheerful mood every day. Five per cent of people have bad moods four or five days a week, and three days of bad moods out of ten is about average. Moreover, people cope with bad moods and sadness and melancholiness with varying degrees of success. Most revealing is the fact that the average person's ability to cope with anger, which is a primary cause of depression, is less effective than coping with daily mood swings.³

Mild mood swings, however, are hardly all most people have to confront. Indeed, the number of people today trying to cope with serious personal problems is staggering. The high divorce rate, the number of people in therapy, the rapid growth of Twelve Step programs, and the increasing occurrence of family violence and violent crimes in general all tell us that we are a people who are in large measure just trying to keep our heads above water. To one degree or another we are a people who struggle with finding meaning in the face of sometimes feeling like we've reached "the end of our rope."

What most of us have heard we should do at any moment we feel this way is to tie a knot and hang on. On the surface tying a knot and hanging on sounds like a good thing to do. The truth is, though, in any difficult situation, momentary or long-term, tying a knot and hanging on is the worst thing we can do for ourselves. As strange as it may sound, we in fact need to do just the opposite. We don't need to hang on. We need to let go! Hanging on makes things worse. It intensifies the frustration, desperation, panic, or sense of things being out of control we may be feeling. The reason it does is because it perpetuates the illusion that we can control the very circumstances that have created those feelings.

Letting go does just the opposite. It takes us to a place deep within that calms us in the midst of the worst possible circumstances. It teaches us about real power and real control; about living authentically without arrogance; about the difference between self-care and self-centeredness; about surrender and victory. Letting go is the way to life, even abundant life! It is an experience that feels like we have been, to borrow a perfectly wonderful biblical phrase, "born again" (John 3:3, 7, KJV), as if we had never really lived before. It teaches us how to enjoy living each day we have because we learn that life is not a rose garden and doesn't have to be. Letting go is the step we take away from trying to control what we in fact cannot control at all. It is the only step that makes real sense, yet it seems to be the last thing we should do. Letting go does not mean we become irresponsible. It means we learn how to be truly responsible.

While I do not want to suggest that I model this kind of letting go, what is written here is rooted in personal experience. Learning how to let go has been the focus of my life for the last five years, and with considerable intensity. The learning has not come easy. I have kicked and screamed all the way. But I now know that it is a hard truth I needed to learn. Yet I doubt I would ever have learned it on my own. That is why I am grateful that I found a little group of people who knew how to let go, and were caring and patient enough to teach me. They did not even know me at the time, but they welcomed me with unconditional acceptance. They offered me no prescriptions or even direct advice. They simply talked about their own experiences of learning how to let go. All I had to do was listen. They spoke a language I understood. At times they seemed to know me better than I knew myself, without ever directly talking about the circumstances of my life. It was not long before I came to believe that a loving and gracious God was speaking to me through them. So I listened more intently, and I began to learn.

A common need is what brought this group together. It was the need we are talking about—to let go. Several of them had been working at letting go for many years. By their own admission, it is not something that one does once, never again having to work at it. But they did know more about it than the rest of us. As time passed I found that a prayer I had heard most of my life was at the heart of what they were talking about, and if I were willing to do what they called "work" the prayer, I just might experience what they had experienced. That prayer has come to be known as the Serenity Prayer. Next to the Lord's Prayer, it may be the most universally known prayer in all the world. It was written by an American theologian named Reinhold Niebuhr in the 1930s. He prayed the prayer at a small New England church he used to attend while vacationing from his teaching responsibilities at Union Theological Seminary in New York. As best we can determine, in its original form the Prayer read:

God give us grace to accept with serenity things
    that cannot be changed;
courage to change things that should be changed;
and wisdom to distinguish the one from the other.

Living one day at a time;
enjoying one moment at a time;
accepting hardships as the pathway to peace.
Taking, as He did, this sinful world as it is, not as
    I would have it.
Trusting that He will make all things right if I
    surrender to His will.
That I may be reasonably happy in this life
and supremely happy with Him forever in the next.
Amen.[4]

One reason the Serenity Prayer has such wide appeal is because it speaks to the universal desire for inward peace. It touches us where we are, and at the same time where we are not, most of the time. It expresses the deepest needs we have—to live with serenity and face change with courage, yet calls us to confess that often we do not know how to do either one. The Prayer offers a simple and at the same time an admittedly difficult way to draw upon a power beyond ourselves on a daily basis. Indeed, its simplicity is so disarming that we can find ourselves saying it without recognizing the challenge of doing what it really means if we are willing to do it.

But anyone who has truly prayed the Serenity Prayer, worked it, knows that saying the words is not enough. In order to experience its power, we have to move from saying it to praying ("working") it. There is a significant difference between the two. Saying the Prayer reminds us of things we tend to forget. Praying the Prayer, on the other hand, connects us with the source of power to live by the words, to give ourselves over to the care of God, the one without whom we can never know serenity, courage, or wisdom.

This difference between saying a prayer and praying one was something I had heard before from Dr. Eberhardt Bethge, who was the closest friend and colleague of Dietrich Bonhoeffer during World War II. While serving as scholar-in-residence at a college where I was chaplain years ago, this giant of a man talked about Bonhoeffer's counsel to the students in the underground seminary of the Confessing Church of Germany to learn to pray the Psalms, rather than just say them. Saying them was nothing more than reading them. Praying them, he told us, meant allowing them to mold and shape their lives. It was in learning the difference between saying and praying the Psalms, Dr. Bethge said, that helped them survive those dark days. It was not until the experience in my group of sojourners that Dr. Bethge's comments began to ring true.

Not that praying the Prayer changes life overnight. It clearly does not. Common to most people is that it takes a long time even to work the Prayer with any consistency. Eventually, though, it does make a significant difference in the quality of our living. When I joined my group I thought I knew how to pray, and certainly how to take God seriously in my life. Yet with their support and guidance I began to reach a depth of experience with God I had not known before. At the same time living by the power of God in the specific ways the Prayer talks about is a journey that lasts a lifetime.

And that is not all bad. Recently I was sitting in a restaurant eating and reading a large book I had just begun. As I looked up for a moment my eyes met a man who was leaving. He looked at the book, then back at me, and said, "You have a long way to go." I replied, "Yes, but the beginning makes me think that it is going to be worth it."

That is what many people have experienced in praying the Serenity Prayer. Though the journey stretches beyond our sight, each day affirms that the effort is worth it. Years ago a friend described living by the power of God as something that continues to get harder and harder and better and better. That says it precisely! Most of us have known the "harder and harder" part. The Serenity Prayer invites us to taste the "better and better" fresh every morning. Not that we are assured of the "better and better" for the future. It is a matter of receiving one day at a time as a gift. This is apparently the way God chooses to work in our lives.

This is precisely the lesson Israel had to learn early. God had promised Moses and the people he led out of Egypt that food and water would be provided daily (Exodus 16:9–31). All they had to do was to trust God to be God. It was not a task they found easy. So when they discovered the manna in the wilderness, they determined that they should gather as much as possible and store it for the next day, in case God failed to provide for them. Having taken things into their control, they learned an important lesson. On rising the next day they discovered the "bread" had been spoiled, and that it could not be stored. They were left to trust God would be God and would do what had been promised. They were called to a trust they found difficult to live by.

It is not so different for us. We are prone to taking life into our own hands, only to learn through bitter experience that we are not able to control life as we would like. Even then we often forget this hard lesson God teaches us. As I write those words I am asking myself why I never experienced the truth and power of the Serenity Prayer before now. Sporadically I probably had, but never on a consistent basis. Why did it take a problem that made me feel like I had reached the end of my rope to make me realize that I did not trust God as much as I thought I did? In retrospect I see now that it was the experience of becoming desperate enough to admit I had reached the limits of my own strength and power that led me to reach out to a strength and power greater than my own, truly reach out to it. Up until then I talked about God, but essentially relied on myself to get through the day. I believed in God, but lived as if I didn't. It wasn't a conscious thing. Quite the opposite, in fact. I was unconscious of how much I was trying to hold on to life in an effort to control it.

Ironically, becoming desperate can turn out to be an unexpected blessing. Someone once told me that desperation can be an ally. It is when we feel desperate that we are willing to try anything to make the situation better— even God! No one likes to feel desperate. Yet when we do, we are usually more open to giving up control, to letting go, rather than trying to tie a knot and hang on! Desperation can be the moment of confronting the reality of limitations and the trustworthiness of faith.

But we don't have to be desperate to learn how to let go. Often a crisis leads us to turn to God, but we can learn to trust God before such a crisis happens. Here is where the Serenity Prayer offers genuine help. Learning to pray the Serenity Prayer is a step-by-step process of giving up the illusion of control. It is a practical way to begin thinking in a new way about ourselves and those we love and those we have to work and live with. It is like putting on new lenses, or seeing things in focus for the first time. The Serenity Prayer works no miracles, but it can make an enormous difference in the quality of our living. It teaches us how to live in a new way.

Part of the appeal of the Prayer is that it simply makes sense. What makes more sense than giving up trying to control what is beyond our control? What makes more sense than focusing on gaining the courage to change what is within our power to change? What makes more sense than seeking wisdom that helps us distinguish which is which? What makes more sense than spending less time trying to keep life under control and more time living it? In a real sense, the Serenity Prayer is preventive medicine, showing us what to do before we reach the desperation point of being at the end of our rope, before we reach the point of discouraging desperation. The Prayer teaches us how to take care of ourselves in healthy ways and how not to try to take care of everyone else. It leads us to be responsible *to* others without feeling like we are responsible *for* them. That is what freedom in God is all about.

The pages that follow are intended to help the reader move from saying the Serenity Prayer to praying it. It is a process of learning how to live inside out, learning how to act rather than always reacting. The Prayer begins with God, and that is where our discussion begins. The chapters on serenity, courage, and wisdom naturally follow. But they are not the whole story. The Serenity Prayer invites us to listen to our feelings, truly to feel them, perhaps for the first time. That is why the chapter on feelings is included.

In searching for a way to describe what happens inside us as we work the Prayer, the metaphor of "dancing" fit perfectly. It captures the essence of the spiritual energy we experience each day we live inside out. To be able to dance is finally to be free. Freedom is the goal toward which the Serenity Prayer leads us. The theme of freedom, therefore, is an appropriate conclusion to the formal discussion of the Prayer.

An Epilogue is included in order to help the reader in the actual praying of the Serenity Prayer. While personal needs and circumstances will shape the way any of us works with the Prayer, there can be value in having specific suggestions that may help us live deeply into it. One practical way to help ourselves do this is to form a small group that will work seriously with the Prayer. Some principles for how such a group can function are suggested. For each chapter, questions that a small group might use are provided in the hope that they might facilitate the process of each person learning to pray the Serenity Prayer and living inside out on a daily basis.

1

God

"God give us..."

It is not just that God can make a difference in a person's
life. It is the fact that what we believe about God, who
we believe God is, can and does make a difference in
our lives. In her book *Will the Real God Please Stand up,*[5]
Carolyn Thomas describes the negative effects of what she
calls "dysfunctional images" that some people have of God.
She is convinced that unnecessary pain and anguish are
caused by these images because they keep people from
knowing the real God, whom she describes as a faithful
God who loves us regardless of our response, a God who
never stops forgiving and nurturing us.

This little book makes an important point for us to think
about as we begin to work the Serenity Prayer. What we
believe about God can have serious consequences when we
take God seriously on a daily basis. It is not enough just to
believe in God. What we believe about God also matters.

The Serenity Prayer inherently affirms God is good,
that God cares about human beings, that God wants the

best for people, that God wants us to have inward peace and effective outward actions. The Prayer reflects belief in the kind of God Carolyn Thomas claims in her book to be the real God, a God who loves us no matter what and never stops forgiving and nurturing us.

The appeal of Thomas' book lies in the fact that she speaks to a general experience of people who have grown up in the church. In its own need to try to control people, the church has for centuries presented "dysfunctional" images of God rooted in fearing God. This fear has been the power the church has used to coerce people to obey its teachings. Many of us have grown up in this kind of church environment. We were not taught about a God who never stops loving and never stops forgiving. We learned, instead, about a God who expects us to get our act together and to keep it together to be acceptable. Not that God's love was not discussed. Only that getting and/or keeping God's love is always dependent upon how "good" we are.

This kind of God is pretty hard to please, and, therefore, we must always watch our step. Of course God doesn't want to reject us or send us straight to hell, but God won't blink an eye in doing it if we fail to straighten up and fly right. "Flying right" means, of course, doing "good" things and not doing "bad" things.

Thank God that most of us now know that this picture of a God who loves conditionally is wrong, all wrong, and always has been wrong. Fundamental to a personal relationship to the God who hears our prayers "yet while we are sinners" is the experience of grace, of love without conditions. The trustfulness of God's unconditional love is made poignantly clear in that most winsome parable Jesus told, the one we call the prodigal son. Yet the way we read this powerful story about a father who loves without conditions, who accepts his sons without them first needing to be acceptable, has itself been conditioned by the picture of God described earlier. Consequently, the parable is often read without our ever hearing its message of grace. Follow me through an extended and careful study of this story to see how its message has been missed—and even distorted—as it has been interpreted through the lenses of the dysfunctional images of God so prevalent today. The parable is usually understood as a story of a father who accepted his wayward son back home when the boy, having reached the end of his rope, repented of his foolish ways. Meanwhile his older brother, being the jealous type, resented the fact that his father not only let his brother come home, but fully restored him back into the family. The message we hear in reading the parable this way is that God will accept us, as the father accepted the prodigal son, only if we repent of our foolish ways and come back home. In other words, we think of this parable as a call to repentance and the loving response of God when we do.

That we should not live irresponsibly, wasting our inheritance as children of God on that which ultimately destroys us, is not in question. But the Serenity Prayer begins with an appeal to grace precisely because grace is never dependent upon the recognition of this fact. The parable of the prodigal is, I suggest, a clear statement that proclaims the startling and even unsettling good news that grace is present before we ever have the chance to make a turnaround in our lives, and that is the reason we have hope in whatever circumstances we face in the first place. This is the story of a father who was willing to risk that love was the strongest force in the world. It is a story that dares to say that God is willing to risk trusting the power of unconditional love with us; that God loves us before we ever love God, and always will; that nothing we do will cause God to withhold forgiveness. It is a story about God giving us what we do not deserve—grace instead of justice, and that is why we can dare to pray.

Am I putting words in Jesus' mouth? I think not. Allow me to lead you through the parable from this perspective so that you decide for yourself. See if you hear the message of grace anew.

The place to begin is to ask the question, "What did the younger brother do the next day?" Perhaps he went to work on the farm? Or is it more likely that he started thinking about how he could get enough money to take off again? He may have come home only long enough to get a night's rest, some food, a few dollars from his overly generous and loving father, and then leave the next day. This is speculative, of course, precisely because the parable is deliberately ambiguous about the boy's real motivations. On first reading verses 17–20a in Luke 15, for example, the prodigal seems to see the foolishness of his ways and, therefore, makes a decision to go home:

> But when he came to himself he said, "How many of my father's hired hands have bread enough and to spare, but here I am dying of hunger! I will get up and go to my father, and I will say to him, 'Father, I have sinned against heaven and before you; I am no longer worthy to be called your son; treat me as one of your hired hands.'" So he set off and went to his father.

Yet if we are honest with ourselves we must confess that many times our actions that are, on the surface, good have a hidden agenda behind them. Was that not possible, if not probable, in the case of the prodigal? Is this an example of genuine repentance, or is the son simply seeing the stupidity of his ways that has gotten him into a bad spot? He has spent all of his money, is working with a hog farmer doing the dirtiest job to be done, is hungry and tired, perhaps discouraged, certainly disgusted with his plight, and then he decides to go home. By his own admission the first thought he had after "coming to himself" in the circumstances he had made for himself was that he knew where he could get food without wallowing with hogs. Rather than assuming repentance here, the best thing that could be said about the son at this point is that he had sense enough to know when, so to speak, to eat "humble" pie.

Moreover, even if he did genuinely "come to himself," in the sense of repentance, it is certainly not an uncommon experience for such a repentance to be short-lived. Conversions sometimes occur at very opportune times, only to fade once conditions change. My own experience in moments of desperation suggests to me that the son's confession of his sins to his father *after* he has reached bottom is the key in understanding the power of the parable's radical message. It is not stretching the parable itself to suggest that at the very least the meaning of the son's "coming to himself" is ambiguous, and is so intentionally. This ambiguity is underscored in the story's next scene. As the son approaches home, his father sees him from a distance and runs out not just to meet him but to welcome him back into the family (verse 20). The father's attitude toward the prodigal is one of love and acceptance. What is more, the father's greeting of the son comes before the son has a chance to say anything. He does not know why his son has returned home, what his motivations are, what his attitude will be in the future. The father lets the son know that he is still a son without knowing anything about his "conversion" experience. When the son tries to make a confession the father really does not take the time to listen:

> But the father said to his slaves, "Quickly, bring out a robe—the best one—and put it on him; put a ring on his finger and sandals on his feet. And get the fatted calf and kill it, and let us eat and celebrate; for this son of mine was dead and is alive again; he was lost and is found!
>
> verses 22–24

The father's response focuses on his own joy, not on the son's intentions or motivations. Coming home is like being lost and then being found, being dead and then having life again. That is cause for joy. This is a response that speaks less about the son than about the father. What the father does in the story is not based upon what the son does or will do in the future, but upon who the father is. What became clear to me as I read this story, in light of my own needs before God, is that at stake here is sonship, and the father's response makes clear that the boy's sonship was never in jeopardy. He is still a son, as symbolized by the gifts the father gives him (verses 22–23).

These gifts are expressions of unconditional love. They are gifts of grace. Certainly repentance is central in the divine/human relationship. But I submit this parable does not speak about repentance. It speaks of grace. It is not about a wayward son, but about a loving God. I think Jesus wants us to hear it as a story about the father, not the son.

The actions of the other son in the story (verses 25–32), and the father's response, also serve to underscore the unconditional nature of the father's love. In many ways the older brother has, in a manner of speaking, gotten bad press. He has been accused of jealousy and lacking a forgiving spirit. But those who understand the brother this way have obviously never been a brother to a prodigal. A truer picture of this brother is one that recognizes that his reaction to the way his younger brother is received back into the family is based upon well-founded suspicions of his brother. He knows that a rebellious spirit is deeply rooted in his brother's heart. The fact is, he knows what he thinks his father does not want to admit, that his brother has some real problems. He thinks his father is being taken in by a son who will end up breaking his heart again, and so he refuses to be party to what he suspects is a charade by the prodigal.

At the end of the story the father goes out to ask him to come to the party. We do not know for sure what the older brother does, but we are left with the impression that he refuses to honor the father's request. His mistake is in not understanding the father's request. All the father asks him to do is to accept the father's freedom to welcome his brother home. But the elder brother is unable to accept the father taking the risks unconditional love sometimes requires.

The actions of the older brother, as those of the prodigal, can be understood to function in the story to reveal the nature of the father's relationship to his children. It is one of grace. But neither one of the sons understood this. In his own way, each misunderstood his own sonship. The younger son thought being a son entitled him to an inheritance that he received at the beginning of the story. When he squandered it he naturally thought his father would reject him. That is why he decided to tell his father to treat him as a hired servant rather than as a son. What he did not understand is that sonship is not something one loses. It is not even something one is supposed to earn or be worthy of. It is simply the nature of the given relationship between the father and son. One can abuse sonship, but one does not cease to be a son. He was the father's son while he was throwing away his life, just as he had been before he left. Coming home had the potential of changing the son's relationship to the father. It did not change the father's relationship to the son.

But the elder brother did not understand the nature of sonship any more than the prodigal did, even though he had remained close to the father while his brother had strayed. He thought he deserved what the father would give him because of his faithful labors. He did not think, as did his brother, that by birthright he deserved his inheritance. He was willing to work for his. Therefore, he interpreted the acceptance of the prodigal back into the family, and possibly a renewed inheritance, as a rejection of his labors, and, indirectly, of him as a son (verses 28–30).

Neither son realized that sonship is a gift. Neither realized that the inheritance the father was willing to give was also a gift neither of them deserved. Neither of them understood the father's relationship to both of them was based upon the father's heart, not their behavior. Neither of them understood the father's grace.

Many people today continue to think like the two brothers. They have not grown beyond the image of an angry God whose judgment is swift and whose punishment is everlasting. Recently I was speaking at a church gathering with other speakers on the program. By design or mistake another speaker was given the same text I had been given. Each of us was to deliver three lectures, and our different perspectives created an unintended point/counterpoint arrangement of presentations. My colleague was convinced that I was not putting enough emphasis on the judgment of God in my lectures. For him the love of God always needs balancing with God's judgment, else we fall into "cheap grace," meaning we live as if God will tolerate anything. This colleague in ministry is quite right in saying that the judgment of God is taken quite seriously in scripture, and is always a factor to be reckoned with in human affairs. But the message of scripture is, I believe, equally clear that God's love not only is unconditional, but has to be for us to have any hope of living in communion with God. Moreover, it is apparent that the early Christians had as much trouble as many Christians today do in accepting the fact that God is willing to take such a risk. In Paul's letter to the Christians in Rome, he responds to the kind of criticism by asking the question, "What then are we to say? Should we continue in sin in order that grace may abound? By no means!" (Romans 6:1). Obviously some of Paul's critics thought he was talking about grace too much and God's judgment too little.

Paul's response was to say that grace produces the kind of freedom that gives birth to genuine gratitude for such divine unconditional love that one lives a life worthy of discipleship (Romans 6:2ff). Indeed, Paul was convinced that encountering this kind of divine acceptance would lead one to allow the Spirit to bear the fruits of righteousness in one's life, rather than leading to one giving in to carnal desires (Galatians 5:13–25).

But the church has found it hard to trust God's unconditional love. Consequently it has preached a God whose judgment is swift and whose punishment is everlasting. This is not the kind of God to whom a person is apt to pray to very often, and certainly not a God to whom one is likely to pray to with much honesty. I am convinced that the church has succeeded in convincing people God's judgment is real, while failing miserably at helping them to trust in a loving God whose grace is steadfast and whose faithfulness is not whimsical. Believing in this kind of God is where prayer begins.

Once we believe in God's unconditional love, we are ready to learn the difference between "saying" and "praying" the Serenity Prayer. What happens is that praying this prayer moves us to take the leap of faith that involves trusting our very survival into God's care without the need to be "good" before we do. We may believe in a God who cares about us, loves us, and wants nothing for us except what is right and healthy. But moving beyond belief to experiencing a sense of divine presence in the circumstances of our lives, a presence that does not leave us, is the effect of praying the Serenity Prayer. In praying the Prayer is, in fact, an affirmation that we believe in a good God, and that we are willing to trust ourselves into this God's unconditional love. This act opens us to experiencing being accepted by God for who and what we are—children of God who desperately need to be received by grace. Paul Tillich once described the sense of being accepted by God unconditionally this way:

> A wave of light breaks into our darkness, and it is as though a voice were saying: "You are accepted, accepted by that which is greater than you, and the name of which you do not know. Do not ask for the name now; perhaps you will find it later. Do not try to do anything now; perhaps later you will do much. Do not seek for anything; do not perform anything; do not intend anything. Simply accept the fact that you are accepted."[6]

Believing we are accepted by God without conditions opens the door to our risking to pray to God in complete honesty. As long as we believe in a God before whom we must constantly "measure up," we will never feel the inward freedom to pray openly and honestly. In our unconscious mind will be the hope that what is "out of sight" will be out of God's mind. Honesty with God is how we have the courage to be honest with ourselves. Unless we can do both, we will not get very far in working the Serenity Prayer.

It is also true, I think, that believing we are accepted by God unconditionally helps us to trust that God is always with us. Believing in a God of conditional acceptance

keeps God at arm's length. It is difficult to trust that someone is always with us, and can always be counted on, when
we feel it is necessary to keep our guard up around them,
when we are never sure whether or not they are going to
accept us. The same is true in our relationship to God. A
God around whom we have to walk on eggshells, so to
speak, is hardly one whom we will trust always to be with
us. It is when we can trust that God unconditionally accepts us as we are, where we are, that we will trust God to
be with us daily.

Trusting that God is always with us means in practical terms that we act on the belief that God will help us in
whatever circumstances we confront. How God helps us
is not easily defined or identified, for the ways of God are
mysterious. At the very least, though, trusting that God
will always help us means being open to experiencing a
strength that goes beyond what we have previously known
as our own. The Serenity Prayer calls upon a power greater
than the one who is praying. In the Prayer the presence of
God is the power of God being offered to human beings.
We pray not only to tell God what is going on in our lives.
Praying expresses the anticipation that the God who accepts us unconditionally will help us. The Serenity Prayer
calls us to a radical trust in God because it is rooted in the
conviction that God is a love relationship that is never at
risk. This conviction moves praying beyond appealing to
a God who needs to be appeased to turning one's life over
to a God who is absolutely trustworthy.

Some people learn early in childhood what it means to
be accepted unconditionally. Some learn this even if some
parts of their childhood hurt and injured them. Unconditional acceptance is being loved when we don't deserve it.
It is being loved when we ourselves do not act very loving,
or even show reckless disregard for the feelings and well-
being of those who are loving us. As children we are selfish. The world exists to meet our needs. Growing up means
becoming mature enough to have the good sense to realize that this is a distorted way of looking at the world. It
takes some of us longer to mature than others. For some

people it seems like it takes a lifetime. But however long it takes us to mature, until such time that we do mature we need a lot of unconditional love, undeserved love—love that overlooks our selfishness and keeps on loving. Parental love is just this kind of unconditional love. Even when conditions seem to be attached to our parents' love for us, down deep the love is really without conditions. They feel it even when they do not always show it. In this age of growing awareness of the damage done to so many children through various forms of abuse, it is important for us to remember that not all parents were or are abusive. Many are long-suffering with their children. Some are even abused themselves by their children, yet they keep on loving. It is in the persistence and stability of parental love that we most often see what unconditional acceptance and love really mean.

The way many children love their parents also demonstrates the human capacity for unconditional loving. The resilience children have in loving parents who have not been good parents at all, who have neglected them, hurt them deeply, and at times have abused them emotionally and sexually is almost an enigma. It is the kind of love that no one deserves, but, then, that is why it is a gracefull love. Some parents do not deserve to be loved by their children, yet are anyway. It is one of the most winsome forms of unconditional love that we ever see.

But even when we do not learn this kind of unconditional love from others, the Serenity Prayer can help us to experience it in our relationship to God. Working the Prayer opens us to the presence of one who always loves us unconditionally, one who desires for us inward peace and effective outward actions. God is where the Serenity Prayer begins. It quickly moves to what we must do for ourselves. But it first calls us to pause and ponder the God who will give us the strength and power to do what we have to do to take care of ourselves. The Prayer begins with God so that in working it we might see God more clearly, love God more dearly, and follow God more nearly, day by day. When we can do this, we not only discover that we are in the presence of a good God, we also discover that we are home:

> When we walk into the unknown it's like walking into a dark tunnel. We do not know what is at the end of the tunnel unless...
>
> By faith we can believe that we will walk into a new beginning, filled with light and hope....
>
> In our changing world there is one who is willing to walk with us through the difficult changes in our lives. In Isaiah [God] says, "Don't be afraid, I am with you. When you go through deep waters and great trouble, I will be with you. When you go through rivers of difficulty, you will not drown. When you walk through the fires of oppression, you will not be burned. The flames will not consume you. I am the Lord. Your God. Your Savior."
>
> Over the years I have had one hope that I can always count on. God will not desert me. When I'm worried about my children and I don't know what to do to help them, I have someone greater than myself to turn to. When people scorn, mock or turn against me, my self-esteem is not destroyed because I am [God's] child, loved deeply and forgiven for all my shortcomings. When my job is like a raging storm, unstable and insecure, I have a promise that the storms will not overflow me and I will stand in the midst of the storm. When my health is broken and I feel weak and broken, I have one I can turn to for strength, power and hope. [God] renews my strength causing me to mount up like the wings of eagles, to run and not be weary.
>
> I have a choice. I can let the situations of this world guide my emotions causing me to live on a roller coaster of feelings. I can be happy when things are going well, and filled with fear and worry when things are not. Or, I can live by faith. Faith that no matter what happens, God is with me.[7]

2

Serenity

*"...grace to accept with
serenity things that cannot
be changed..."*

Serenity is the pearl of great price in modern society.
Whoever could bottle and sell it would quickly become
rich. It is the conscious or unconscious center of all
human craving or desire. The search for it has made
therapy the boom business it has become in the last
twenty-five years. People want serenity, peace of mind, a
sense of inner tranquility and calm, a feeling that all is
right with the world. We spend millions of dollars every
year trying to buy it. Nothing much in life feels quite right
without a sense of serenity. The more complex, compli-
cated, and confused the world around us has become, the
greater our longing for serenity. The wish for simple days
long passed, when neighbors knew neighbors and had time
to talk to each other, when we did not fear letting our children play outside, when communities were communities,
when families actually sat down together for meals, the
search for love and joy and hope—all of these are, I believe, expressions of the modern quest for serenity.

Years ago a rabbi named Joshua Loth Liebman wrote a book entitled *Peace of Mind* and it became a bestseller. Several newspaper columnists used the book as a basis for articles they wrote over a period of several months after its publication. It was hailed as "a brilliant attempt to uncover the wellsprings of happiness, and to lead the patient toward mental health."[8]

If anything, the quest for peace of mind has only intensified in the time since its publication. The problem with our quest for serenity, though, is that most people are looking for it in all the wrong places. There is an old legend that one day the gods were gathered by the chief god, Brahma, who declared that because they had so abused it, the divinity of humans had to be taken away. He inquired of the other gods where to hide it. They suggested that it be put on the highest mountain. Brahma replied, "No, for one day humans will learn to climb to the highest mountain and claim it for themselves again." Then place it at the farthest corner of the earth, they said. But, again, the answer, "No, one day they will reach to the farthest corner of the earth and claim it for themselves." Then put it in the deepest point of the ocean, the council of the gods declared. Brahma replied, "No, for one day humans will plummet to the deepest point of the ocean and claim it for themselves once again." The council sat for days and not one of them knew where to hide the divinity humans once possessed. Then Brahma spoke again, "I know where we shall hide it. We shall place it deep within humans themselves. They will spend their lives climbing to the highest mountaintop, traveling to the farthest corner of the earth, and plummeting to the deepest point in the ocean, but will never find that which lies within their reach deep within themselves." And so, the story says, it was done.

Telling this story is not intended to suggest that to possess serenity is to become divine, but only underscores that serenity is a pearl of great price, and we seem to stop at nothing in search of it. Yet all our searching has yielded at best temporary peace that has evaporated, as if a vapor. The reason is simple enough to see—we are looking for serenity in all the wrong places—in everything and anything the "good" life will yield to us: education, power, prestige, sex, entertainment, even therapy, all to no avail. The futility of our search seems to intensify our panic over not finding what we are looking for, longing for, what we desperately need in order to feel our lives really do count for something. What we have yet to recognize is that we have become imprisoned by the worst illusion of all— that if we work at it hard enough and long enough we can shape life into the way we want it to be and then we will have the pearl of great price, the serenity our hearts desire. Once we entrap ourselves within the illusion that we can control our lives, we naturally take the next step and begin to try to change whatever needs to be changed in order to form life as we need for it to be.

It is an illusion, you know. It really is. Life cannot be controlled as we imagine. Few things are within our capacity to form and shape as we want them to be. But our need for serenity pushes us to cling to control ever more tightly, pushing serenity further from our grasp. In the first line the Serenity Prayer confronts us with the ultimate illusion, that we can change whatever we have to change to have it. It just is not true. The Prayer is telling us that the opposite is the case, that only when we realize that we cannot form and shape life into the way we want it, that only when we realize that there are some things— if not most things—that cannot be changed, then and only then do we have any chance at serenity.

It is an illusion most of us have a lot of trouble giving up, even when we say that we know better. We are not unlike the man in the old story who went to see his doctor, moved his shoulder up and down and said, "Doc, every time I do this my shoulder hurts." His doctor replied, "Well, then, don't do that." The message of the Serenity Prayer is not unlike that "doctor" saying to us—stop doing that to yourself. Stop beating up on yourself. Stop doing what makes you hurt. Stop hitting your head against the brick wall of reality. Stop searching for serenity, for peace of mind, in your efforts to control, change, or manipulate life into what you want it to be. You are looking in the wrong places. What you desire is to be found in giving up your illusion that you can control the world and people around you.

Trying to change what cannot be changed in our lives amounts to self-abuse. We abuse ourselves emotionally, physically, and spiritually every time we ignore the truth of this first part of the Prayer. Most of us learn this truth the hard way. That there are some things in life that we cannot change may be one of the painful lessons we learn in life, if we ever do. Until we do we put ourselves in a sure no-win situation where the only possible outcome is pain. That is self-abuse. We ought to stop doing it to ourselves. The truth is, we can. Why? Because of a fact of life underlying the truth of the Serenity Prayer—we have a choice about the way we live. We can waste time, energy, and even money trying to change what cannot be changed in our lives, or we can choose to accept those things as they are. Either way we are making a choice. Control is an illusion. Having choices is real.

The wife of one of my colleagues helped me to understand how true this is. Two years ago she experienced life-threatening heart problems that led to surgery and a long road to reasonable recovery. We were talking about how we allow people and things to upset us. She said that she no longer had that "luxury." Getting upset drains her of energy to the extent that she has no strength at all. For example, she said, if she is taking a walk and a car cuts her off at a corner, she must choose not to let that upset her or she will not have the strength to get back home. She has learned to clear her mind of upsetting thoughts as she walks. For her it is a matter of choice, in this case a choice to live.

What this spiritually mature friend lives with daily is what all of us live with in reality—choosing the quality of our living. Most of us do not experience the urgency of making the right choice as she does. Yet the choice is no less important, if any of us wants to enjoy meaning-full living. Recognizing this fact can help us to identify—and confess—some unhealthy ways we act and react in my life. We may, for example, be a "fixer." If there is a problem at home, we "fix" it. If there is a problem at church, we "fix" it. If there is anything that needs changing, "fix" it. Some people spend a lifetime "fixing" things. It never seems to occur to us to ask whether or nor all our "fixing" is actually needed or helpful, or possible! We seem to live on automatic pilot—we see a problem and zoom in to "fix" it. "Fixing" becomes a way of life. Any time "fixing" something is difficult, or appears as it really is—impossible, we blame the something.

Few of us make it through life without facing some serious problems. With so much practice in "fixing" little problems, we are programmed to tackle the big ones as well. It usually takes an elephant-size problem to "fix" before we realize that what we are doing is not fixing anything, and may even be making things worse. The real problem, of course, that we face is never what we think it is. It's not what we think needs fixing that's the problem. It's our thinking we can that is the real problem. We may be confronting a genuine problem, to be sure, one that is full of pain and hurt and much worry. But we are only adding to it by becoming spiritually, emotionally, and even physically unhealthy because we will not accept what we cannot not change. Our hope lies in the first line of the Serenity Prayer. There we confront the truth. We have a choice. We can accept what cannot be changed, or we can keep on living in an illusory world.

What an obvious, yet freeing, insight it is to realize that how we live is up to us, that we can choose to react to people and circumstances in a way that is healthy or unhealthy. The choice belongs to us. This does not mean that everything in our lives will be as we want it to be. It never will be. But we can learn that life is better when we accept the fact that what we do when facing things that cannot be changed is a matter of choice.

That the quality of our lives is a matter of choice seems to be one of the great secrets of life. There seem to be only a few people who learn early in life that the way they live, the quality of their living, is a personal choice and nothing else. This is, I submit, an axiom of life applicable to any and all situations. Not that there are no circumstances that are unjust, unfair, horrible, hurtful, or that we should never raise a protest against inequity and inequality. It is only to say that ultimately, and finally, quality of life is a choice.

What better public example do we have of this great truth than from the witness of one who suffered from injustice most of us will never know. When Nelson Mandela was released from his South African prison after twenty-seven years, he did not come out a man embittered toward life. He came out as a man still committed to justice and equality for blacks and whites in his native land. His imprisonment alone did not make him a hero. Nelson Mandela's character made him a hero. That character was rooted in the wisdom that how well one lives is a matter of choice.

There is an intimate relationship between serenity and choice. Serenity is a choice—nothing more, nothing less. If we do not realize this simple truth, we shall never have it. But the degree and levels to which we resist it have a way of being obvious and hidden at the same time. Let me cite a personal story that illustrates how this truth plays out in simple, ordinary experiences. When I accepted my present position, the seminary needed a picture for the announcement. Not having one, I went to a local department store that was running a special. Having my picture taken is not my idea of fun under any conditions. The cartoon of the father slowly losing control as he tries in vain to take a family picture with an automatic camera, with everything going wrong that could go wrong, is the way taking pictures has always been for me. This time was no different. After waiting an hour and a half while the photographers played with all the babies brought in by adoring mothers to have their pictures taken, I concluded that my time was more valuable than that, so I left—fuming at the people in charge who could have taken at least three hundred pictures of me while they were getting one of the babies and their mothers.

All the way to the office in my mind I wrote a letter I wanted to send to the store and the picture company telling them what happened and what kind of incompetent people they had working for them. When I reached the office I was ready to explode. My staff could see that it was not a good idea to be around me for a while. As I sat and simmered it dawned on me what I was doing—trying to change something that could not be changed. I realized that it was "choice" time. Hold on to what happened or let it go—the choice was mine, and my serenity, not to mention sanity, was at stake.

That incident helped me to see other incidents, mostly silly, where I refused to accept my inability to control. Seasonal changes in the weather, for example. I want the weather to be what it is supposed to be in its season. Winter, as strange as it may sound, is my favorite time of the year. I live where it is supposed to be cold in January, but warming in March. It was warm in January. It's March now, and we just experienced the blizzard of the century. Spring and warmth seem very far away. It would be easy to let this get to me to the point where I make myself miserable. What could be more obvious than that? Yet it is only when I stop to think about it that the absurdity of my resistance to accepting that fact becomes obvious! Then I realize that my serenity in this situation is my choice.

If not being able to change things like the process of getting a picture taken or the weather frustrates and upsets us, what about the important things we face that we cannot change? We simply have to accept the fact that in situations of little significance or great, choice and serenity are inextricably linked. They are two sides of the same coin. Choice determines the level of serenity. The size of the problem does not determine whether or not we have a choice. We always have a choice.

The first year I came to my present position I found myself in a relationship of tension with a student. Whenever we were in the same room there was a tension between us that I am sure we both felt. I found myself going out of my way to avoid her. I felt as if she had not given me a chance to get to know her before she made up her mind about what kind of person I am. It bothered me a great deal. I would find myself thinking about her dislike for me at all hours of the day and night. It took several weeks before I realized that I was allowing her behavior to hook my need to be accepted into a new community, and, therefore, I was unable to see the obvious—that I could not make her change her opinion of me. Finally I realized that I had a choice. I could try to change her, or I could accept the fact that I could control my reaction to her. I chose to let go of her and do something about me.

This kind of experience happens to us all the time. A woman I know works with a man new to her company whom she simply does not like. At first she allowed him to disrupt every work day. She went home upset and frustrated, ready to quit. Finally she realized that she was hurting herself by the way she was reacting to him. Nothing she could say or do was going to change him. She had to decide whether or not she was willing to accept that fact, or continue to make herself miserable, and quite possibly end up quitting her job. She chose to work on herself. She has not learned to like him any more than she did at first, but she has chosen to focus her thoughts on her attitude rather than on what he does that upsets her so much. In others words, she has accepted the fact that serenity in this situation is something she has to choose to have. It is true in every circumstance of life.

What has been said about the relationship between serenity and choice also holds true for serenity and expectations. Serenity and expectations are inseparable. It has been said that the level of one's serenity is inversely proportional to the level of one's expectations, which means that more expectations produce less serenity. There is an inevitable trade-off. The greater my expectations in a situation the more frustrated I will be when they are not met, and the greater the temptation to intensify my efforts to make the situation conform to those expectations. A circle of frustration develops at that point—expectations lead me to try to change what cannot be changed, which makes serenity impossible, which makes me more frustrated with the situation, which makes me try all the harder to change it, which—and on and on.

⌣ This does not mean that expectations are inappropriate. It is simply to say that expectations have no power to make anything happen! On the negative side, they have the potential of warping our sense of reality, creating false hopes that fly in the face of the limitations we have as human beings. In and of themselves expectations cannot make anything happen. What we expect of others has no inherent authority. This is why religious legalism ultimately fails to shape behavior. Expectations have to be accepted voluntarily to have authority, otherwise they collapse under their own weight. The frustrations and anger we often feel when others do not conform to our expectations should serve as a clear indication of our resistance to accepting things that we cannot change.

One expectation we sometimes struggle with is that others will understand us as persons—who we really are. Everybody wants to be understood. I do. You do. We all do. It is basic to being human. It bothers us when we think someone has misunderstood something we have said or done. We don't want them to get the wrong opinion about what kind of persons we are. When this happens it always hurts and upsets us. The Serenity Prayer leads us into accepting our limitations in controlling how others react to us. Eventually we reach the point where the hope that others will understand us will not control us.

Not that we stop caring about what others think of us. We continue to hope that people will understand our words and actions. But we can choose to accept the fact that we cannot control them. Instead we can start asking God to help us to do what we believe should be done, and to love people whether they understand us or not.

A wall-hanging in my office reads:

I know you believe you understand
what you think I said; but I am not

sure you realize that what you
heard is not what I meant.

The fact that we know what we say and what others
think we say is often very different does not diminish the
frustration we feel. It seems such a simple thing to expect
that people would hear what we say. But everything we
say is filtered through the needs and wants and feelings
of the hearer. That reduces the chances of actually being
understood. Even "yes" and "no" are often not heard in
the way they are meant. Someone gave me a business size
card I now carry with me that says,

Just what is it about
NO
that you don't understand?

The simplest statements are misunderstood and mis-
construed. Most of us have played the circle game in which
the leader whispers a sentence to the next person who
does the same thing, and so on, until it comes back to the
leader in a version quite different from the way it started.
That is the way life is. People do not always hear what
other people actually say. This is especially true in situations of stress or crisis. When emotions run high, commu-
nication problems are exacerbated. Sometimes we say
things in such a way that they are easily misunderstood
or taken the wrong way. The miscommunication then becomes our responsibility. Yet in normal circumstances, and
certainly when the situation feels stressful, even the
clearest statement can be misunderstood and miscon-
strued. We help ourselves to live with this fact of life by
giving up the expectation that we will always be understood, and receiving it as a serendipity when we are.

The relationship between expectations and serenity
also cuts both ways. Not only do our expectations of others destroy our serenity; so do the expectations others have
of us. This is where the problem of "people pleasing" can
control what we say and do and try to be. People often say
that they don't care what other people think. Personally I

don't believe a word of it. We do care what others think, and well we should. All of us have a basic need to belong to others, to be where people know our names and seem to be glad we are there, where we feel accepted and liked. Flipping our noses at people's opinion of us is simply a way to try to avoid the hurt we feel when they don't accept or like us. What others think of us is important for our own well-being. But when our self-esteem begins to depend primarily upon what others think, we put ourselves into an emotional prison. We lose our individuality and the freedom to make decisions for ourselves. Serenity is impossible because we are constantly worrying about what someone else may be thinking of us.

A young man once told me that he spent most of his time trying to please other people. No matter what the conversation, he ended up telling them what he thought they wanted to hear. Others knew this to be the case and grew suspicious of everything he said. They learned the hard way that he would often tell one person he agreed with something they said or did, and then tell someone else with an opposite point of view that he agreed with them, always in attempting to please everyone. He experienced serious job and marital problems because of his excessive people-pleasing behavior.

This is an extreme case, but it points to a danger all of us face. Some of us have greater "people-pleasing" needs than others, but all of us like to be liked enough to try to live up to the expectations of others. The issue is whether or not we do it to the point where it becomes an unhealthy need. A dominant need to please others hinders acceptance of things we cannot change because we are not confident enough in who we are to live with unresolved problems in relationships.

What is important to see is that the relationship between serenity and expectations is one of control. Control is the basic issue in refusing to accept what cannot be changed. Being in control is a demanding and exacting need. To feel like we have no control in our lives can create a sense of panic. But the perception of having no control is an illusion. We do have a measure of control in all situations. The issue is what kind of control it is. No one can control situations and people, which can be a terribly frustrating fact of life. Many times the situation we want to control needs some control, needs some changing. My boss may be a jerk. My neighbor may have no consideration for other people's property. My children may do things that hurt them. My marriage may be falling apart. All of these situations and/or people may need changing. But that does not give us any more control. It simply magnifies our need for it.

We do, however, have control over one person—ourselves! If we choose to, that is. Under no circumstances are we ever helpless. We may be powerless; we are not helpless. Powerlessness means not being able to make life the way we want it to be. Helplessness, on the other hand, is refusing to do the best we can with what life gives us. When we confuse the two we fail to see how much could be done with the way things are. Recognizing the difference between having control *in* and having control *over* our lives is a sign that we are willing to work the Serenity Prayer rather than just say it.

Trying to change what cannot be changed, then, is a choice. So is accepting what we cannot change. That choice comes down to this—are we willing to let go of things over which we hold no control? In other words, are we willing to admit that we are not God? Here is where it really gets tough. Letting go, especially if it involves someone we love, is just about the hardest thing in the world to do. No one finds letting go easy. Love makes it that much harder. In many instances letting go feels impossible. But it only feels that way. It really is possible. It is possible when there is one we can let go to.

There is an old, amusing story about a man who fell over a cliff, managing to grab hold of a small tree growing out of the side of the mountain as he was going down. There he hung. After he collected himself he yelled down to the bottom of the canyon, "Is anybody down there?" only to hear the echo of his own voice reverberate back to him.

So he looked up and yelled, "Is anybody up there?" to which a reply came, "Yes, my son." He responded, "Well, can you help me?" Again a reply, "Yes, my son, just let go." The man yelled up again, "Is anybody else up there?"

The story underscores a simple but profound truth. Help comes from God by letting go. It sounds overly pious to say that, but it is true nonetheless. Human extremities are God's opportunities. This is why the notion that we should tie a knot and hang on when we reach the end of our rope gives the wrong message. It is precisely in doing the opposite—letting go—that we find solid ground upon which to stand. As long as we are clinging to where we are, trying to hang on by our own strength alone, trying to pick ourselves up by our own bootstraps, we have no open hand with which to reach out for help.

Letting go is possible for the believer because we have someone to whom we can turn over loved ones and situations. This is why the Serenity Prayer assumes faith in God. The comfort of believing in a good God to whom we can trust people and situations we cannot control is real. Not that God will simply take care of everything the way we would if we did have control. It is that we trust that a power greater than ourselves is at work for good in the situation. Without knowing the outcome, it helps to believe that God is present in all our troubles. It is what makes real and lasting serenity possible.

Accepting things we cannot change and accepting them with serenity are hardly the same experience. We may have the strength, perhaps stubbornness, to stand back and not rush in to do something about a situation, if we set our mind to it. But that is not letting go with serenity. It is only when we let go to God that our thoughts don't race, our insides don't churn and our stomach doesn't get messed up. Doing this enables us to accept our limitations as a part of being human. We feel more confident about letting go because we don't feel like we are leaving everything to chance.

Letting go to God is perhaps the only effective way we have to cope with worry. Worry is always a sign that we are holding on to what we cannot change. It is a common experience to catch ourselves worrying about something we have been trying to control right in the middle of something else we are doing. How many meetings—even worship services—have we sat in while our minds are absorbed by troubles and problems we supposedly let go?

My children becoming young adults has made me see more clearly how reliable worry is in telling me I have not let go to God. I made the decision to let them go by thinking that their mother and I had done the best we could to provide the kind of environment children need in which to grow up with self-esteem and lasting values. Now it was up to them. So I let them go. At least I thought I did, until they started making some decisions I didn't like. I didn't step in and try to force my choices on them. I really had accepted the fact that I could not do that anymore. But I spent a lot of time playing the "what if" game— "What if it's the wrong decision?" "What will happen if...?" Finally I realized that worry was telling me that I really had not let go of my children. I had accepted the fact that I was powerless to control the decisions they make, but I was acting like I was helpless to take the next step and really let them go into the care of God. That meant trusting that the values we had tried to instill in them would serve them well as adults.

Letting go of children is a frightening experience. There are times when we feel afraid for them, no matter their age. But if we practice the Serenity Prayer, we are sure eventually to taste at least a bit of the wonderful experience of being released from the responsibility for making everything "right" in their lives. We think it is when they have grown up. In truth it is when we finally do! Growing up is finding out that we are not ultimately responsible for the happiness and well-being of our children, our friends, our lover, our spouse, the people with whom we work, or anyone else. The real self-deception is thinking that people we try to make happy just won't survive unless we are always there trying to make things right, keeping things on an even keel and straightening out all the messes.

Letting go is never easy. But what a relief when we do. As painful and difficult as it is, it is in every situation the best thing we can do for ourselves. We do not suddenly stop caring about what is happening. We simply choose to accept our limitations as the place where God becomes even more real. This is how we receive the gift of serenity, even in the worst of circumstances.

Frederick Buechner poignantly describes in his book, *Telling Secrets*, his experience of finding serenity in letting go of one of his daughters who was suffering from the eating disorder *anorexia nervosa*. His daughter, he says, simply stopped eating. She did not do so in a dramatic way, as if she were trying to draw attention to herself. In fact, her motivation seemed rather typical. She thought she would look better if she lost a few pounds, so she cut back on her diet. As the months wore on, though, and her diet became meager indeed, then the situation became very alarming for her family.

Buechner sought information about *anorexia nervosa* and found that it relates to young people (the group most likely to suffer from it) wanting to be free and independent and at the same time wanting to be safe and taken care of. *Anorexia* satisfies both of these longings. Not eating symbolizes staking out one's claim to independence, while the weight loss and subsequent weakness creates a response of care and concern from others. This kind of thinking may sound illogical, but the disorder is commonplace nonetheless.

Buechner's daughter grew thinner and weaker. He says she eventually had the appearance of one of the victims of Buchenwald. He grew more and more afraid and sad, and felt more and more helpless. She would not respond to any effort to reason with her or persuade her to start eating. This daughter he loved so much was steadily committing suicide right before his eyes, and he couldn't do a thing about it. Her fear of gaining weight outweighed her fear of dying.

Buechner makes no attempt to tell her story, why she did what she did and what she was thinking about. He tells his story alone. It is enough for all of us. For what he realized in this struggle was that he was, in his words, starving to death as much as his daughter was. He wasn't living his own life any more because he was so caught up in hers. In a strange way she was better off than he was. She had consciously given up food. He had given up nourishing himself, but he was a long time in realizing what he was doing. The word he uses for his own situation is *Hell*. Hell is where there is no light, only darkness. He was so caught up in his fear for her life that none of the usual sources of light in his life were working. He did things he had always done. His wife and other two daughters were beside him, yet none of it brought light to his life.

To be at peace, he says, is to have peace inside yourself more or less in spite of what is going on around you. That is precisely what the first part of the Serenity Prayer is saying. But Buechner had no peace at all. His emotional state responded directly to her behavior. While scripture says, "Perfect love casts out fear" (1 John 4:18), he says his fear for his daughter had cast out love. Love was being consumed by anxiety. For the only thing he knew to do was what he had been taught to do—to take care of his daughter. He was ready to move heaven and earth to make her well. He couldn't, of course, but he was not ready to hear that, so he continued to try to change what he could not change, control what he could not control, cure what he could not cure. He could see that anything he did on her behalf seemed to stiffen her resolve not to eat, but he continued to try.

What saved him, and possibly her, was when she had to be hospitalized while she was three thousand miles away from home. Society stepped in through doctors and nurses and a judge who determined that she was a danger to her own health and ordered her admitted to medical care. Little by little, far removed from her father's efforts to make her well, Buechner's daughter began to eat and regain her strength and health. And the lesson for him? His own words say it best:

If your daughter is struggling for life in a raging torrent, you do not save her by jumping into the torrent with her, which leads only to your both drowning together. Instead you keep your feet on the dry bank—you maintain as best you can your own inner peace, the best and strongest of who you are—and from that solid ground reach out a rescuing hand. "Mind your own business" means butt out of other people's lives because in the long run they must live their lives for themselves, but it also means pay mind to your own life, your own health and wholeness, both for your own sake and for the sake of those you love too. Take care of yourself so you can take care of them. A bleeding heart is of no help to anybody if it bleeds to death.[9]

Holding on, refusing to accept what one cannot change, control, or cure seems to be a loving thing to do. It is an illusion. Inner peace requires letting go. Life will not be lived any other way.

> To a dear one about whom I have been concerned.
> I behold you lovingly in the care of the Father.
> I release you from my anxiety and concern.
> I let go of my possessive hold on you.
>
> I am willing to free you to follow the
> dictates of your indwelling Lord.
>
> I am willing to free you to live your
> life according to your best light and understand-
>   ing.
> Husband, wife, child, friend—
> I no longer try to force my ideas on you, my ways
>   on you.
> I lift my thoughts above you, to a
> spiritual being, created in his image,
> and endowed with qualities and abilities that
>   make you needed, and important—not only to
>   me but to God and His larger plan.

I do not bind you. I no longer
believe that you do not have the understanding you
need in order to meet life.
I bless you.
I have faith in you.
I behold you in Jesus.[10]

Letting go to God—it has a "bumper-sticker" sound to
it, but it is not a "bumper-sticker" way of living. It captures the essence of accepting with serenity things we cannot change.

We, of course, would like to have serenity all the time.
More likely is experiencing serenity one situation at a time.
The fact that we may have been able to let go once does
not mean we are able to do so in all circumstances. The
common experience is that each time we confront things
that cannot be changed we are tempted to try anyway,
even though we may have accepted a previous situation.
Not only does serenity come one day at a time; it usually
comes one situation at a time as well.

One reason it is so important to realize this is the case
is because we often get down on ourselves for not being
able to accept what we cannot change immediately in all
situations. We think that if we did it once, we should be
able to do it again. We can, but it will always require a
conscious effort to do it in each situation.

Moreover, serenity not only comes one situation at a
time. It also comes one day at a time. It is all we can do to
have it one day. What we discover, though, is that living
one day at a time is a sane way to live. One day is usually
manageable. More than that can be overwhelming. When
we try to handle more than one day we often end up han-
dling none. But when we take things one situation at a
time, one day at a time, we find out that God's grace is
sufficient for the day, and through God we can do all things
at least some of the time.

3

Courage

*"...courage to change
things that should
be changed..."*

What is the worst thing somebody could say about you?
For me it would be, "Don't mind Jan. He's always
been that way." How sad it would be to live in such
a way that people would think that we had always been
the way we are, that we had never changed, never grown,
never developed, never learned from mistakes, never accepted new ideas. Such a person is among the living dead.
It was Thoreau who wrote that he had gone to the woods
to see if he could learn what they had to teach so that
when he came to die he would not discover that he had
not lived. To be described as someone who has always been
the same is to be a person who has not really lived.

It helps to think of the relationship between serenity
and courage as sequential. That is, courage follows serenity because serenity calms us down enough to see things
from a different perspective. Trying to change things that
cannot be changed, at least not by us, keeps us stirred up.
We feel desperate inside and have no capacity for having

a balanced perspective on life. Serenity changes all this. It brings focus to our lives. We are able to see things that we simply could not see before, and to see what we can see only with "sane" vision. This is why serenity precedes courage. Only as we see things clearly can we have courage to do anything about them.

The word *courage* means "the quality of mind that enables one to encounter difficulties and danger with firmness or without fears." One might question the "without fear" part. Indeed, true courage may be to do what needs to be done even in fear. We don't have to be unafraid to be courageous. Serenity opens our lives to God's power, which makes it possible to act, whether we are afraid or not. It positions us to have the strength to make the changes that need to be made. Courage is the will to act. The place to start is with the person we look at every morning in the mirror.

But let's not get ahead of ourselves. Knowing that we need to do some changing usually leads us to think of all the things that are wrong with us. Well, there are things wrong with us. At the same time there are many things right with us. The wrong things simply get in the way. We shall discuss this in detail later. For the moment it is important to put weaknesses and strengths in their proper context. That context is learning how to be. The most difficult thing we can do is to be. It takes courage. Many of us don't like who we are, so we don't want to be at all, certainly not who we have to be.

For this reason having the courage to be requires a healthy dose of self-love. Most of us know and even desire that we should love our neighbor as we love ourselves. That means, of course, that we cannot love our neighbor if we do not love ourselves. A person who cannot love herself or himself has limited capacity really to love others. Their love will be self-absorbed, seeking to find their own worth in others. Much can happen to us early in life that so injures our self-image that we grow into adulthood believing that we are not people of worth. Many of us hide our true selves from others for fear that if they discovered who we really were, they would not like us.

Self-conceit is a problem for some people, but the truth is there are just as many people for whom self-contempt is a greater problem. Our trouble may not be that we love ourselves too much. It is that we love ourselves too little. Lack of self-love often shows itself in at least one of two ways. The first is that we spend all our time trying to make the world the way we want it. We are overly critical of others in order to hide our self-contempt. What has been called a superiority complex, which means a person acts like they are better than everyone else, invariably stems from low self-esteem. The other way self-contempt shows itself is total lack of concern for one's own health and well-being. Low self-esteem makes it difficult for us to take care of ourselves in appropriate ways. When there is no sense of self, there is nothing to take care of. Consequently there are no boundaries that give a person the personal space needed to be who she is.

The effect of both of these types of behavior is the same. There is no capacity to have the focus or energy to do something about the things we can actually do something about. Self-love precedes making the changes we can make because any change we can affect begins with us. The one thing we can always do something about in our lives is ourselves. Serenity prepares us to focus on ourselves by helping us get comfortable with ourselves, love ourselves, reject any notion that we are not persons of worth. Healthy self-respect gives us the courage to make changes that need to be made in us to better our situation. Specifically, those changes have to do with attitudes and behavior. Let us begin with attitude.

Attitudes affect everything in life. As one person has said:

Our attitudes are truly the lenses of the mind through which we perceive reality. However, there is a comparison which helps me more fully understand the force of attitudes. I imagine our attitudes as jurors sitting in the jury box of the mind, poised and ready to interpret all the evidence that is brought before them. These juror-attitudes are ready to pronounce verdicts and to suggest appropriate actions and reactions.[11]

Attitudes determine what "verdict" we pass on each situation we encounter daily; they determine whether or not our actions and reactions are appropriate; and we are responsible for them, not someone else, not something else—we are responsible—because *our* attitudes make the decisions.

The good thing is that attitudes can be changed. They are never set in concrete unless we choose to pour it. In a sense we can put some new jurors in the box. They are not there for life. The key is having the courage to make the changes. Yet a common problem among us is clinging to unhealthy attitudes. Moreover, we seem to convince ourselves that we deserve them, that we have a right to wallow in them and get as muddy as possible. But when we get up and look at ourselves, we see the mess we have made. It is then that we can realize how foolish we have been. We are the ones who get dirty and we are the ones who have to clean up the mess.

Attitudes can be changed! Look at this picture. What do you see: a woman whose face is stern or a woman whose face is pleasant?

Both are there. Think of the picture as a mirror into which you are looking to see your dominant attitude about life. The stern expression represents negativism; the pleasant expression represents positivism. In

every circumstance in life the positive and negative co-
exist. We choose to view situations from one perspective
or the other. At the same time, our attitudes influence what we see.
What we see is generally determined by where we stand.
Attitudes are part of where we stand. And to a large extent what we "see" is usually what we get. If we see a
glass half full, it will be. If we see it half empty, it will be
that way. Or, as comic George Carlin says, we can see a
glass that is twice as big as it needs to be. This does not
mean that our attitude causes us to see things that are
not there. It means only that our attitude always prevents
us from seeing everything that is there, whether it be negative or positive.

This has come home to me in a very personal way. A
brother of mine was an active alcoholic for many years.
His drinking became a barrier to our enjoying a good relationship. Once I took a group of college students on a silent retreat. The theme for the weekend was being peacemakers. Silent retreats have a way of bringing issues to
the conscious mind when we least expect to be thinking
about them. That happened to me on this retreat. On Sat-
urday afternoon I realized that I could not lead my students in thinking about being peacemakers unless I was
willing to make peace with my own brother. The next week
we met for lunch and I did just that. After our meeting I
was able to think of him as my brother "no matter what."
This is not to say that his behavior no longer bothered me.
It did, not only for the pain it brought to all of us who
loved him, but because he was wasting away a talented
life. I simply accepted the fact that only he could change
himself. What I could do was to change my negative attitude toward him, and in doing it I changed the way I reacted to him.

A negative attitude is a demon of the first order. It is
responsible for much of the misery we experience. What
is worse, it is very contagious. Negative thinking, like negative news, spreads like wildfire, while the positive has to
fight for survival. People complain about so much nega-

tive news on TV and in the papers. The fact is, it sells. The more sensational the negative news is, the more it sells. Put two stories on the same page, one positive and one negative, and the negative one will be the one people remember.

Because it is so contagious, it takes courage to refuse to get caught up in negative thinking. This choice means marching to the beat of a different drummer. A man I met years ago was very intelligent, and such a successful businessman that he had taken early retirement in his mid-fifties. He was fascinating to be with. But his worldview was shaped by a simple, very negative attitude. In his own words, "People are OK until they get together, and then they are not worth a damn." It is tempting to surrender to this kind of attitude. It comes down to choosing the kinds of attitudes we want to live with.

A primary obstacle in choosing a positive attitude is to think of ourselves as victims of the circumstances of life. Many people do. They confront problems already defeated by thinking they are victims of the unfairness and injustice of life. The "woe is me" way of thinking soon dominates them, and then their unhappiness or misery or pain becomes someone else's fault. They see themselves as pawns on the chessboard of life. Things are beyond their control. They get caught up in a cycle of despair where negativism feeds playing the victim and playing the victim deepens the negativism.

Victims always lack the courage to change their attitudes because they think the cause of problems is external. They look outside themselves for solutions. That usually means something or someone else has to change. Certainly not them. They have convinced themselves that their happiness or peace of mind or joy in life is dependent upon anything and everything but themselves. They refuse to see that they make their lives what they are to a degree far greater than they want to admit.

We can choose not to think of ourselves as victims by realizing that victims are prisoners of their own attitudes. Playing the role of a victim is a self-imposed limitation on what we can do with our lives. No one can do anything about the limitation except ourselves. And there are more than a few examples of people who have made this choice. If one can, any of us can. Consider, for example, the story of Belinda Mason.

Belinda lived in Hartford, Kentucky, with her husband and two children. On September 9, 1991 she died of AIDS. When she gave premature birth to her second child through a difficult cesarean section, she was given several untested pints of blood. Soon thereafter she tested positive for the HIV virus. A year later she was diagnosed as having AIDS. If anyone had the right to think of themselves as victim, it was Belinda. Yet she refused to do so. She was appointed to the National Commission on AIDS, traveling far and wide to educate the rest of us about it. Two years before she died, she said of her situation: "I would not trade places with any person. My life is abundant. And I continue to be highly blessed."[12]

Belinda was a positive-minded person who flatly rejected the temptation to play the role of a victim. She knew she had the choice to live or wait for death. She chose to live. Each of us has the same choice. We can change the way we think at any moment. We have control over that part of our lives. We may not be able to change the external situation, as in the case of Belinda Mason, but we can change the way we think about ourselves in the face of it. Our attitude is up to us. Life is not fair, and many tough situations are not of our own making. But it is up to us to decide whether we let them defeat us or whether we rise above them.

As our attitudes change, so does our behavior. We can do something about how we act as well as what we think. We do not know which influences which: whether a better attitude helps us act better, or whether acting better helps us think better. Psychiatrist William Glasser has built an entire therapeutic process upon the empirical principle that people can act themselves into a new way of thinking.[13] And before Glasser came along, the founders of Alcoholics Anonymous, Dr. Bob and Bill W., discovered they could stop drinking long before they changed their way of thinking.

Someone has said that there are three kinds of people in the world: People who let things happen; people who make things happen; and people who wonder what happened. People who do not believe that they can change things in their lives are the kind who let things happen, and in some instances sit around wondering what happened. People who make healthy things happen, on the other hand, realize that they have choices in life. They can change their actions and reactions.

Some people are content to be spectators. They watch life go by. But people who make things happen participate in life. They are unwilling to sit in the bleachers and let others play the game. They want to be on the field. They know that the game can sometimes get rough, but they want to be involved. If we accept the Serenity Prayer for the challenge it is, there is no room for being a spectator in any situation. The Prayer is as much about change as it is about acceptance. Moreover, having the courage to make changes is as difficult as accepting things I cannot change.

This is especially true because of the resistance of others, even those closest to us, to changing our actions and reactions. It is not uncommon to have someone say, "I don't know what's happened to you. You're not the same person you used to be." What they do not know is how right they are. By choice we are not the same. We have decided to take control of what we have some control over—our attitudes and actions. But they do not know how to react, so they do what is understandable. They try to get us to go back to old ways so we will be our "old" selves.

Resisting other people's resistance to changes we are making is not easy. We may find ourselves second-guessing decisions we once thought were right. Sticking to those decisions will require much courage. The Hebrew people who came out of Egypt had among them those who, in the face of adversity, became voices of resistance to the new life that lay before them. They longed for the familiar and the known, even though it represented bondage. These voices of resistance at times were able to convince the rest of them to turn back, to give up the road to a new life. Such voices are always persuasive. They also represent that which once held us in bondage.

Becoming a person who makes healthy things happen for yourself may mean choosing to leave a situation that is unhealthy for you. That kind of decision, especially if it involves a marriage and family, is extremely difficult to make. Immediately you confront the voices of old tapes running in your head telling you the do's and don't's of life. These, coupled with the voices of the other people who are affected by your decisions, can become a throng of resisters to what is healthy for you. Listen to them. Give them a fair hearing. But in the end ask for the courage to make the healthiest decision you can make for yourself. I believe healthy decisions are the right ones. Sometimes what others think are the right ones are far from being healthy.

Becoming a person that makes healthy things happen will mean that you stop taking care of other people who need to take care of themselves in order to be healthy emotionally, spiritually, and sometimes physically. This usually involves making some tough decisions, such as the one that faced a woman whose granddaughter was addicted to heroin. The granddaughter had been in and out of several treatment centers, without lasting recovery. Her grandmother finally made the decision to stop rescuing her every time she called for help. Most of the time her granddaughter wanted a place to stay when she ran out of friends willing to pay her way. When the day came the young woman was stunned by her grandmother's decision. She accused her of being callous and uncaring. Her granddaughter's words made a deep wound, but this wise grandmother stuck to her decision. It was a courageous moment for her. It reflected a will both to accept what could not be changed and to change what could be.

There is a story that brings these first two parts of the Serenity Prayer together in a memorable way. The son of the well-known minister, Dan Polling, was a young chaplain in the Navy during WW II. In the last letter he wrote to his dad before his ship went down in the Pacific he said, "Dad, I want you to know that I am not afraid. I only pray that God will help me think right so I can do right so I can be right."

That is what the Serenity Prayer helps us do. Serenity helps us think right; courage helps us do right; and both enable us to be right. Serenity calms us down, helps us regain our balance, puts problems in perspective, and clears our heads. Courage moves us to action, helps us to focus our energies in the right places, and empowers us to make the tough decisions life requires us to make in difficult circumstances. Serenity and courage—the roots and the fruits of letting go rather than hanging on.

4

Wisdom

*"...and wisdom to
distinguish the one
from the other."*

Somewhere I read that "everyone is a fool at least five minutes a day; wisdom is the ability not to exceed the limit." There may be no better, certainly no more graphic, definition of wisdom than this one. The word itself means to have good judgment in the face of the demands of life, to possess discernment of inner qualities. No doubt to stay within the five-minute limit will take this power of discernment, and more!

There is a well-known, even well-worn, story about a young man who wanted to test the wise man of his village that is worthy of being told again. The young man placed a dove in the palm of his hand and went to the wise man to ask if the bird were alive or dead. If the wise man said it was alive, the young man would squeeze the bird to death. If he said it was dead, the young man would open his hand let the bird fly free. "Old man," he said. "Is this bird in my hand alive or dead?" Gazing into the young man's eyes, the wise one replied, "It is as you wish."

The Serenity Prayer intrinsically defines wisdom. It is knowing when to accept things and when to change them, when to squeeze and when to let go. Until we can make this distinction, living from the inside out is not much of a possibility.

But how do we get wisdom? How do we become wise enough to know when to accept things and when to change them, when to squeeze and when to let go? Not an easy question to answer. Perhaps the starting point is to realize that we do not become wise by trying to; we do not find wisdom by looking for it. I want to suggest that it is by and large a by-product of something else. What that "something else" is may be debatable. I think it has to do with learning the obvious in life. Wise people see what is—and has been—in plain view that others do not see and, if they do, do not recognize as significant. The truly wise know that one of the primary sources of wisdom is common sense.

A counselor friend once made the remark that the increasing role of the modern therapist has been commensurate with the decreasing role of the next door neighbor. The point being that many, if not most, people who seek counseling just need someone to talk to; and if they have a problem, most of them already know what to do, or not to do, about it. They just need to hear another perspective by which to test their own perceptions. The reason they know what to do is because in almost any situation all that is needed is a little common sense. Counseling may help us understand better why we do what we do. It certainly helps us work through what we are feeling. But in the final analysis most of us don't need counseling in order to know what to do in tough situations.

It may be that the loss of trust in common sense has been one of the casualties in the rise of "the tyranny of the expert" in modern culture.[14] People today think important problems require "expertise." Consequently, they look to the "expert" for information and answers. Although experts render invaluable service to society, the fact remains that common sense is more needed than it ever has been.

In the face of problems endemic to modern society, one might make a reasonable case that the experts have done about as much harm as good. A good dose of good old common sense could probably do as much good in most situations as all the expertise that could be gathered. The point is not to blame experts for our problems, but to suggest that wisdom is usually as close as the good sense all of us possess. The Serenity Prayer is common sense wisdom—don't waste time and energy trying to change something you cannot change in the first place; and do not fail to change something that not only should but could be changed. The truth is that most of us know which one is which. Our problem is not that we do not recognize things we can and cannot change. It is, instead, doing it.

The most profound truth is usually the simplest, and everyone can recognize it. Common sense is the power to recognize the simplest truths of life. Socrates once said that wisdom was knowing that you do not know. Simple. True. Profound. In my opinion—common sense. Ancient teachers of wisdom said that reverence for life was the beginning of wisdom. Simple. True. Profound. Jesus of Nazareth said that we should treat others the way we would like to be treated. Simple. True. Profound. Common sense. The Roman philosopher, Epictetus, said that our problems were not what bothered us, but the way we looked at them. Simple. True. Profound. Common sense. Wisdom is more than common sense. But common sense is always wisdom.

I once spoke to a group about trusting their common sense to know what and when to accept and what and when to change in their lives. All of them responded by saying they had never thought of wisdom as using their common sense. But that made sense to them. And well it should. The connection between common sense and wisdom is an obvious one. Common sense is our God-given sixth sense. It helps us "look before we leap," to state another bit of commonsense wisdom. If we didn't do anything but that—looked before we leaped—many of us would be a lot wiser in most situations.

One of the most popular books of recent years has been *Everything I Really Need to Know I Learned in Kindergarten*, by Robert Fulghum.[15] The title comes from an essay he wrote by the same name that took a fortuitous route to a publisher's desk, who immediately recognized its appeal. Everything Fulghum said he learned in kindergarten was commonsense stuff—share everything; play fair; don't hit people; put things back where you found them; clean up your own mess; don't take things that aren't yours; say you're sorry when you hurt somebody; always flush—all of it down-to-earth truth simple enough for a child to understand, yet profound enough for an adult to live by.

Common sense may be the best guide available for making daily decisions. Sometimes we reach the end of our rope because we don't use it. We do everything wrong in trying to deal with a serious problem because we don't use it. We panic in tense situations because we don't use it. We say things we should not say and do things we should not do because we don't use it. Common sense is the great equalizer in life. It is something everybody has, and the measure given to each is enough for the day. That is all anybody needs.

A second source of wisdom that closely follows using common sense is what might be termed old-fashioned "trial and error." Even as we try to make the best decisions we know how to make, mistakes are made. Letting go of those things we cannot change and taking hold of those we can is not an exact science. Trial and error sometimes can reveal the foolishness or wisdom of our thinking or behavior in very effective ways. It is not a bad thing to have to learn from our mistakes, and it is a very good thing to discover that we were wiser than we realized we were in dealing with a problem.

The best that any of us can hope for is that we will do the best we can under the circumstances we face. That means there will be times when we find ourselves holding on when we need to let go. Wisdom is not always seeing ahead of time what to do. It is also recognizing mistakes when they are made. Foolishness is to keep repeating the mistake. Trial and error is not a time to scold ourselves for making a mistake. It is an experience to be used to grow wiser. The fact that hindsight is 20/20 is why it is such a good teacher!

The older we get the truer it seems that wisdom comes through living for those who do learn from mistakes. Indeed, the mere passage of years yields important lessons that simply cannot be learned any other way. Aging for most people is more than a matter of growing physically older. It is also a process of becoming wiser in knowing what can and cannot be changed, and in the capacity to accept the former with serenity and face the latter with courage. In a culture that exalts youth, as a society we do not value the wisdom that grows in us through living as we might. But the failure of society as a whole does not prevent us on an individual basis from drawing upon this important source of wisdom.

That living yields wisdom is why the writings of the ages are so important. Certainly for Jews and Christians the Bible—and commentaries on it—are an indispensible resource of wisdom. But the writings of the ages in almost every field of human endeavor can serve as teachers for those of us in the modern age. The human effort to find meaning and purpose to life, and to live as fully as we can live, did not originate with the twentieth century. It would only make sense that we who would seek to be wise today in the art of living would reach back to the wisdom of those who have gone before us to learn the lessons of history that might help us along the way. George Santayana observed that those who do not learn from the mistakes of the past are destined to repeat them. That can be true on an individual as well as a collective level. The wisdom that comes through a lifetime of living in one person is a composite of that which is to be found in the writings of the ages, and it is within the reach of our fingertips every day.

A third source of wisdom, and the one the Serenity Prayer underscores most clearly, is God. The Prayer requests God to grant us wisdom. This petition goes to the heart of what it means to trust in a power greater than

our own. In spiritual terms this is called "discernment."
Discernment grows out of faith in a God we discussed earlier, who intends only good for us and works on our behalf
to help us experience it. Thus, discernment is our effort to
pay attention to God. Such paying attention involves something that is not easy for most of us to do. It involves "waiting."

The importance of waiting for God is discussed with
great clarity and inspiration by Sue Monk Kidd in her
book *When the Heart Waits*. She talks about a point in her
life when she believed God was inwardly working in her
life to help her claim her truest self, but she was being
asked to wait to see what the fruit of that work would be
and where God was leading her. But, as she says, she didn't
want to wait. For her it seemed to be "the rawest kind of
agony."[16] She was, by her own admission, impatient with
God and anxious for whatever change she was experiencing to get done!

During this period of internal struggle—and fermen-
tation—she traveled to Saint Meinrad Archabbey for a retreat. One day she went for a walk after morning prayers,
but could not remain still at the edge of the pond where
she had sat down. As she was returning to the guest quar-
ters, she saw one of the monks sitting perfectly still beneath a tree. Later she sought him out and said, "I saw
you today sitting beneath the tree—just sitting there so
still. How is it that you can wait so patiently in the moment? I can't seem to get used to the idea of doing nothing."

She said the monk broke into a broad grin and said to
her, "Well, there's the problem right there, young lady.
You've bought into the cultural myth that when you are
waiting, you're doing nothing." And then he said, "I hope
you'll hear what I'm about to tell you. I hope you'll hear it
all the way down to your toes. When you're waiting, you're
'not' doing nothing. You're doing the most important something there is. You're allowing your soul to grow up."[17]

That is a word all of us need to hear. We are, as Sue
Kidd describes us, a generation of "quickaholics."[18] We

want what we want instantaneously. We are not a people given to waiting. Waiting feels like we're wasting time, getting nowhere, doing nothing. That is often the way it feels to work the Serenity Prayer. "Working" the Prayer leads to "waiting." Spiritual maturity, which working the Serenity Prayer leads to, is not a fast track. Impatience, therefore, comes quickly. It is then that commitment to personal healthiness is truly tested. The Serenity Prayer does make a difference in the quality of our living, but that difference develops over time. We have to be willing to work and to wait. As someone has put it, there are no instant grapes in God's vineyard. We are susceptible to discouragement when we think there are.

Waiting does lead to discernment. That is the witness of Christians through the ages. Elaine Prevallet describes this process as the indwelling Spirit of God giving us the "nudge" we need to know what to do and not to do in decision making.[19] For her the waiting for discernment leads to "listening" for decisions, rather than "making" decisions.[20] This is more than weighing pros and cons. It is trusting that in waiting we are led to "sense" what it is God is guiding us to think or do.

Our resolve to remain constant in this "work" of waiting can be greatly strengthened if we do it within the context of a community of faith where we are valued and loved, nurtured and at the same time held accountable for the wisdom we say we want to have. It is in community that understanding is deepened and faithfulness is nurtured. It is in community that we find out other people experience the same struggles we experience. Spiritual intimacy with God grows when we share spiritual intimacy with others. It was in community that I discovered the wisdom and power of the Serenity Prayer, and gained the courage to work it. It may be possible to work the Prayer alone, but it is a work made unnecessarily harder. The strength found in community can never be matched by what we can do on our own.

It is usually within the context of participation in a community that we are able to find a particular person with whom we can talk openly and honestly, the kind of person who in scripture is called a "faithful friend":

> Faithful friends are a sturdy shelter;
>   whoever finds one has found a treasure.
> Faithful friends are beyond price;
>   no amount can balance their worth.
> Faithful friends are life-saving medicine;
>   and those who fear the Lord will find them.
>
> Ecclesiaticus 6:14–16

One translation says, "A faithful friend is the elixir of life" (RSV). I like that, for faithful friends are the best there are in human relationships, and they are rare indeed. Some of us have been fortunate to have been blessed with some very faithful friends through the years. I have two people who have been this kind of friend to me. Let me tell you about both by describing something of the faithful friendship I have had the longest.

Our friendship is now twenty years old. As my faithful friend, I know without any question that she accepts me unconditionally. Though we live in distant cities, she is always present—truly present—with me by phone or letter when I need her, and never once have I ever felt any judgment or rejection from her. She does on occasion say things that I do not want to hear, but our friendship is never at risk. The bond holding us together is too strong.

Several years ago she sent me an article by newspaper columnist Colman McCarthy about men and women who share a faithful friendship. He wrote:

> Someday I'm going to put aside the day's chaos and take time to report the details of a love story between a woman and a man who were not lovers but friends. If sexual love is a dosage of intense feelings, a widening of veins that let the emotions pass unclogged from heart to heart, friendship can permit a rarer sensation: raising affections higher than the passingness of the emotional. The woman

and man I would write about were friends because
their closeness was based on distance. They could
stand back.

It was either an Irish mystic or poet, and it's usually one or the other, who said that a friend is someone who knows the song in your heart and plays
back the words when you forget how they go.[21]

Judith is this kind of faithful friend to me, an elixir of
life, a rare treasure indeed. I cannot say for sure what
makes this kind of friendship possible in all circumstances.
For us it was the presence of the divine Spirit. My friendship with Judith began within the context of spiritual direction. Through the years we have valued friendship
above everything else. I believe that God has always tran-
scended our being together. This friendship is a gift of God.
We do not create it. We simply have to try to be faithful to
it.

Everyone needs a Judith, but not everyone is a Judith.
Faithful friends know how to listen, how to speak, when
to do which, and to keep on loving through it all. This is
what separates these relationships from other relationships. Not everyone has the wisdom to be a faithful friend
to another. Some of the worst advice is given by well-mean-
ing friends and family members who have the will, but
not the wisdom to help another. In a faithful friendship
advice is secondary to the relationship. Faithful friends
are more interested in listening than in being heard. They
do not let us off the hook when it comes to making decisions. Neither do they leave us to face the consequences
alone. They are always there for us. Because they are who
they are, they help us grow in wisdom.

The nature of a faithful friend relationship means that
we can disclose ourselves in complete honesty. There is
general agreement that self-disclosure to a significant
other is an essential element to emotional healthiness. In
his book of several years ago, *The Transparent Self*, Sidney
Jourard says that a healthy personality means having the
capacity to make one's self fully known to at least one other

significant human being.[22] At the same time, he says, self-disclosure is a means of achieving a healthy personality. This is because people stop growing when they repress themselves, never letting anyone fully know them. A faithful friend is that "significant other" to whom we can make ourselves fully known because we can trust ourselves fully to our friend. This is a relationship that is a divine gift.

Sometimes the kind of trust and support and help found in a faithful friend relationship can in some measure be experienced within the context of a "faithful" support group. The group that has helped me learn how to work the Serenity Prayer is such a group. Its members are ordinary people who are trying the best they can to live under difficult circumstances. We meet for the sole purpose of sharing our experiences in trying to live the Serenity Prayer. Our guidelines are simple and effective. No one judges anyone else's situation, no one offers unsolicited advice, no one tells anyone what to do about problems. The members of this group make a conscious effort to listen, to support, and to share pieces of their own story. In the process a group wisdom and power are created that strengthen and nurture and guide each of us. Any of us alone may not be very wise in knowing when to squeeze and when to let go, but all of us believe that this group keeps us from being more foolish than we might be.

Why is there such group wisdom among these friends? Perhaps there are several reasons, but one of them has, I believe, something to do with the capacity of the "old timers" in the group to live authentically, genuinely, with no pretense or show. They come together not to impress each other but, in a sense, to press together, to stand close to each other so they can hold each other up. They know the meaning of the words:

> Two are better than one….For if they fall, one will lift up the other; but woe to one who is alone and falls and has not another to help.
> Ecclesiastes 4:9–10

What happens in community, in small groups, and with faithful friends is that as we grow in wisdom, at the same time we also grow in our capacity to love unconditionally. An unloving, uncaring wise person is a contradiction in terms. A person may be intelligent, but without caring for others such a person is far from wise. This is because wisdom needs a good heart as well as a good mind. Loving people are not always wise. Wise people are always loving. They seek to discern the way in which love is best served in situations, and then conform their thoughts and actions to support the power of love.

The wisest people are usually ones who are very encouraging of others. The Quaker philosopher Elton Trueblood has been for so many people through the years among the wisest of this world. When he speaks, others listen. Yet his wisdom has never separated him from those less wise. What has always seemed to matter most to him was not to impress others with his wisdom, but to be an encourager to others. One of his protégés, James Newby, published a book of Trueblood's essays by the title *The Encourager*.[23] He exemplifies the wisest of the wise in his love of people and concern that they develop the talents and gifts they possess.

The truly wise also realize that healthy love is not a doormat. It can be as tough as it is tender. Acceptance and change need both. Love that runs from accountability is unhealthy. It is an enabler of irresponsible living and damaging situations. Unhealthy love always leads to trouble. Healthy love recognizes when there is trouble and then empowers us with clear thinking to make difficult decisions. It knows how to reject destructive behavior without playing God by passing judgment on the person. Healthy love is, in short, wise love.

As I look back over the years that my family tried to cope with my brother's alcoholism, it is clear to me now that we did all the wrong things because we did not believe in tough love. We thought love meant rescuing, and that is what we tried to do. It was not easy for us to learn that love that always rescues also enables people to continue in their problems. It is something all of us need to learn if we want to be people who know when to squeeze and when to let go.

5

Feelings

Praying the Serenity Prayer gives us the power to refocus attention on our attitudes and behavior—knowing what not to do and what to do. When you have reached the end of your rope, gaining your balance is the only way to be able to make healthy decisions.

Yet being human means that we are more than what we think and more than what we do. We also feel. Feelings influence how we see what we see. They influence our actions and reactions, the wisdom of the decisions we make, and the sense of hope or despair we have about situations. Feelings are, I suspect, the primary reason we will or will not work the Serenity Prayer. More than anything else they knock us off our feet.

We often get bogged down in negative feelings. It only takes a word or a moment's experience or a special day to throw us into what a friend of mine calls a "grand funk." When this happens we get down emotionally and stay there until the blues pass. What usually precipitates this mood is facing a situation we cannot change, such as spending a holiday alone, not getting a job we wanted, or coping with difficult family circumstances. It is not easy to pray the Serenity Prayer at such times. If we wait until we feel like it, we probably will not pray it. Yet it is precisely at these times that we need to work this prayer. What we must do is to learn how to cope with our feelings in a healthy way so they will not keep us from taking care of ourselves emotionally and spiritually. What that means is that we have to identify our feelings and then find appropriate ways to express them.

I think it is helpful to distinguish feelings from emotions. It may seem to be an artificial distinction, but in reality separating the two describes more accurately the way we experience them. I suggest thinking of emotions as the waves of the ocean; feelings as the water. Waves rise and fall, rush in and recede. The water is constant. It is the real force behind the waves. Feelings are the force behind emotions. They are always present. Emotions rise and fall, rush in and recede. Feelings are constant. A person who is emotional does not have more feelings than one who is not. All of us have feelings. Some of us show them, some of us do not. The absence of degree of emotional expressions does not reveal the presence or absence of feelings, any more than heavy waves in contrast to calm ones reveal the presence of water. Everyone has feelings, expressed openly or not. Feelings and emotions are interrelated, but distinguishing between them can help us understand the constancy of the former and the movements of the latter.

It is also helpful in learning to express feelings to accept the fact that feelings do not have morality, that is, there are no right and wrong feelings. As children we heard the words, "You shouldn't feel that way." The message conveyed was that some feelings were right and some were wrong. Consequently, when we had the "wrong" kind, we felt guilty about it. The guilt in turn caused us to try to suppress our feelings. Some people suppressed all feelings, not even distinguishing between what they thought were good and bad ones. Someone has said that guilt is the gift that keeps on giving. The more we have feelings we think are wrong, the more guilt we feel, and the more we suppress those feelings. The guilt remains because the feelings remain.

Feelings do not have morality, except as we choose to nurse them in ways that are destructive to us and others, as we shall discuss in the next chapter. Even then, the issue is not one of right and wrong, but what is healthy and unhealthy action. Feelings themselves are not right or wrong. What we decide to do with them may be. But feelings are like the air we breathe. They keep us alive. Having them is both normal and healthy. They are one of the common denominators among human beings. It does not matter who one is or what one's station in life may be. Feelings are radically egalitarian. They are no respecter of persons.

Accepting the fact that feelings do not have morality will depend in large part on the extent to which we have experienced God's unconditional love. If God is important in our lives, this is the beginning point for having the freedom to admit feelings, and to feel them without remorse or guilt. Unless and until we trust that we are accepted by God no matter what feelings we have, we will never be free to acknowledge what we feel. The fear of being unacceptable to God because we have certain feelings can become an obstacle for serious praying. Experiencing inward wholeness is rooted in being free from the fear of God's rejection. The freedom to feel our feelings in the presence of God is important. Not to fear God means having the courage to identify negative feelings. Until we do this we cannot do anything with them or about them. We cannot heal them.

Feeling our feelings means being conscious of what is going on inside of us. As we are, our feelings can become our teacher. This is one of the important functions of feelings. If we pay attention to them, they teach us about ourselves. They reveal what often remains unconscious or unacknowledged. As long as we are afraid of our feelings, we cannot learn anything from them. When we accept them as normal and unavoidable, they show us what is in our hearts.

Do you know what kind of heart you have? When I have asked people this question it has usually given them pause. Many of them confess that they have never really thought about what kind of heart they have. Nor have they understood feelings as windows through which they can look into their hearts. Feelings can teach us so much about ourselves because they are half of who we are. The other half is what we think. If we know what we think, we know half there is to know about ourselves. The "feeling" half is the rest of the story.

I once attended a workshop that focused on feeling feelings. At the beginning of each session the leader would do what she called a "feeling check." She went around the room and asked each person to give one word to describe what that person was feeling. It was revealing to see how difficult it was for us to identify our feelings. Most of the time we would describe what we were thinking. She pushed us to name our feelings. The problem we had in doing this indicates how "unschooled" we are in dealing with feelings, and certainly in learning from them.

There is a certain amount of anxiety that is unavoidable when we first start working with our feelings. This is why it is so important to do it in the context of prayer. To be able to trust that we are not alone as we move into unknown territory, into an area that may "feel" like a wilderness, is essential to having the courage to keep going. We will be tempted to go back to denying or ignoring what we feel. When we start praying the Serenity Prayer in earnest we quickly realize that we are on a road most of us have never been on before, which causes us to feel very vulnerable. Praying this prayer in earnest leads toward acknowledging feelings we may not have even known we had. It is not uncommon when this happens to feel like we don't even know who we are anymore. At that point it becomes very tempting to give up the journey to a new self-awareness. What keeps one going more than anything else, though, is the capacity to trust that one is being led by God on this path to a new reality.

Our hope lies in the fact that in the context of prayer feelings can be "reformed." The workshop mentioned above was called a "reforming feelings" weekend. It was conducted within the context of religious faith. The focus was on naming and acknowledging feelings in order to reform them. Actually it could have been described as letting feelings be transformed. We discussed opening ourselves to the power of God to reform—and even transform—our feelings. The point was that it is the power of God that does the reforming. The experience of knowing we can bring our feelings as well as our thoughts to God is essential to them being healed, transformed, reformed.

A woman came to talk about her college-age daughter being on drugs. The problem had been going on for over a year, but she had never talked to anyone about the situation. She felt like she was reaching a breaking point. One of the first things we had to deal with was her guilt about her anger toward her daughter and her husband who was denying their daughter had a problem. She felt ashamed about the way she felt. She said that she sometimes felt like she hated both of them. But a good Christian, she thought, shouldn't feel that way.

When we finished talking the tensions in her visibly diminished. It was amazing to see the effect on her of finally expressing her anger. She began to think more clearly about the things she was doing that were making the situation worse. The decision she reached that day was to attend an Al-Anon meeting the next night. But the real value of the conversation was that she had found someone to whom she could express her feelings and at the same time be affirmed as a person. In the ordinary experience of someone listening to her she discovered that she was living in fear that her anger made her a bad mother and wife, and, thus, that she was unacceptable to God. Simple affirmation of her as a good person no matter what she was feeling helped her think and feel in a different way about herself and the situation she was in. At the same time, my assurance of God's unconditional love for her was as if she had heard the "good news" for the first time. Once she began to believe in God's acceptance of her—no matter how she felt—a visible change occurred in her.

A healthy coping with our feelings is to know that we can name them in the assurance that we are being held in a relationship of love with God that is never at risk. Divine acceptance and help are strong enough to empower us to accept and change things in our lives even when we are afraid:

> Even though I walk through the darkest valley,
>   I fear no evil;
> for you are with me;
>   your rod and your staff—
>   they comfort me.
>
> Psalm 23:4

Once we experience the freedom to name and acknowledge our feelings, we are better able to find appropriate ways to express them. Feelings we know are there but are not expressed build up inside until they explode, hurting us and others. That only makes us feel worse. A woman not long ago talked about letting her anger build up and then it exploded, leaving her feeling very guilty about the way it came out. Yet she had every right to be angry. Her father was facing open-heart surgery with the prospects of survival marginal. Even though she accepted the fact that her husband could not, or would not—and she wasn't sure which—travel with her to her dad's, she did expect him to call and show some interest and concern. But he didn't. He never called, and never asked her how she was doing after she called him. She did not let him know for several days how upset she was. Finally her anger got the best of her, and she really let him have the full force of it. Even though she needed to get it out, it left her feeling worse rather than better because of the way it happened. That is what happens when feelings, especially anger and fear, remain unnamed and unexpressed. Negative feelings do not evaporate.

In the book *The Long Gray Line*,[24] which is the story of
the 1966 class of West Point, Rick Atkinson tells of an
incident that poignantly illustrates this point. Cadet
George Crocker's father died during his freshman year at
the Academy. His family had called to tell him to come
home, and when George asked if his father was still alive,
he was told yes. When he arrived home he discovered that
his father had already died. Family honesty had been
important in the Crocker family, and George was very
angry about not being told on the phone that his father
had already died. He chose not tell his mother how he felt,
though, until several months had passed. When he finally
did, he discovered that his father, in fact, was alive when
he first called home. He had forgotten about the hour's
time zone difference between New York and Nebraska,
which accounted for his thinking that he had not been
told the truth about his dad's death. Unable to express his
hurt, he had carried unnecessary anger that had impeded
his healing.[25]

Whether or not you pray the Serenity Prayer—really
work it—depends in part on your willingness to identify,
feel, and understand your feelings without feeling guilty
in the process. We cannot not have feelings. The most constructive thing we can do for ourselves is not hide from
them. We need to cry and talk and sometimes fuss and
cuss. It is part of being human. Men need this and women
need this. Feelings have no sexual preference. Everyone
thinks and everyone feels.

Unacknowledged feelings often lead us to hang on to
the rope until it is too late to let go, that is, until the situation has gotten the best of us. This is because we are not
able to open ourselves fully to God. This allows those feelings to jerk us around, which makes us hang on to the
rope even tighter.

Friends who know me well will smile at my saying all
of this. They know that I know what I am talking about,
not because I have been able to feel my feelings easily.
Just the opposite. Because I have not. I have learned the
hard way. Acknowledging my feelings as I have faced stress

and problems has been a long process for me. It remains a struggle. I remember actually saying to a friend that I did not have time to deal with my feelings. I had too many responsibilities to take the time to get into that kind of "stuff."

I did just that for many years. It finally caught up with me. My true feelings would not be denied any longer. I had played a game with myself of always being in control and on top of things. I told myself I could handle anything. As I look back now such an attitude seems naive and foolish. At the time I thought it made sense. I wonder now how I could have thought that. But I did. Finally feeling my feelings released me to examine why I had become such a people-pleaser, to which my need to fix everything gave expression. Had I not heard through the support of others that it was OK to acknowledge my feelings openly and honestly, I suppose I would still be unaware of the patterns of unhealthy behavior I was following.

Some of us may never really be comfortable in dealing with feelings. The fact that we know we must has itself become one of those things we have to accept with serenity. Many people are more comfortable in the external world than in the inner world of feelings. But all of us have to learn to accept the fact that our emotional well-being depends on our staying in touch with our feelings.

One practical suggestion that has proven helpful to many people in naming and expressing feelings is to keep a spiritual journal in which to write about the struggles that accompany turning life over to God. Journaling helps us apply the Prayer to specific situations and circumstances by acknowledging in complete candor our thoughts and our feelings. In writing we have moments when we experience what the Quakers call "clearness," which is another word for "discernment." Journaling crystallizes thoughts and feelings. Sometimes we do not realize how confused and fuzzy our thoughts and feelings are until we attempt to write about them. Struggling to find words that express thoughts and feelings reveals what we are actually thinking or feeling. My own experience in journaling regularly for over twenty years is that I am surprised again and again by what journaling reveals to me.

Sometimes journaling becomes little more than a discipline to be followed. Everyone experiences dry periods when the practice seems to be little more than following a routine. Years of experience, however, suggests that staying with journaling always bears good fruit eventually. Part of the reason this is the case is because journaling is a practical way for us to position ourselves to attend to what is going on inside us in a way that nothing else does. Years ago a spiritual director told me that he journaled during dry times because he knew eventually something would start happening again, and he wanted to be there when it did.

That is precisely what journaling is all about. It positions us to be there when something is going on in us. It is a way for us to be present to ourselves. Moreover, I often find it to be the single most effective way I know of to pay attention to the power of God at work in my life. Denying feelings directly affects one's spiritual life. Unacknowledged feelings create mixed motivations in a relationship to God. The ego constantly gets in the way of living a life immersed in the will of God. It stands in the way of turning our lives over to God's will as we discern it. Indeed, the wise ones in my little group frequently remind the rest of us that the word *ego* can mean "easing God out."

Learning how to admit feelings and grow in self-love without becoming self-indulgent is a serious danger when we first begin to face our true feelings. It is quite common for people to become so caught up in acknowledging their feelings for the first time that this is about all they can talk about. They are self-absorbed in their pain or hurt or newfound freedom to the point where every conversation focuses on them. We can be telling them something that has happened to us or expressing feelings we need to express, only to realize that the conversation has shifted back to them.

Self-indulgence is a danger whenever we risk being honest about our feelings. One way to guard against self-

indulgence, though, is by bringing feelings into consciousness within the context of prayer. That is precisely the
reason the Serenity Prayer is so important. It is a prayer
that raises our consciousness about what we feel, but in a
way that is healthy and constructive. The Prayer puts us
in the posture of seeking after a right spirit in the circumstances we face. We are able to feel our feelings and at the
same time pray:

> Create in me a clean heart, O God,
>   and put a new and right spirit within me.
>   Psalm 51:10

Naming and acknowledging feelings in the context of
God's unconditional love frees us to admit the extent to
which we often live through our needs. Doing this takes
us a step beyond feeling feelings. Becoming conscious of
the fact that we live through needs means recognizing that
how we relate to others involves more than what we are
feeling in the moment. Needs are windows into our past.
They tell us about the ways in which past experiences have
shaped who we are. Thus, how we respond to another person can be significantly influenced by these deep-rooted
needs. Further, what we need from others often leads us
to impose unreasonable expectations on them. Until we
break through the web of feelings we are having, we do
not recognize the extent to which we do impose expectations on someone else. When we do sift through our feelings, we are then able to weigh the legitimacy of the needs
that prompt such expectations. We are balanced enough
to discern which needs can be met by others and which
needs must be dealt with internally.

More often than we realize, we love other people
through our own needs. That is, we love them as a way of
feeling good about ourselves, arising from low self-esteem.
But healthy self-esteem is something no one can give to
us. Consequently, we are disappointed, or even angered,
by the way the person we love responds to us, not because
the response is inadequate, but because their loving us
cannot fulfill our need for higher self-esteem.

This distinction between naming and acknowledging feelings and living through our needs is a subtle, but important one. Once we feel our feelings, we realize it is our responsibility to deal with them. Expressing them often helps us do that. On the other hand, being unconscious of the extent to which we live through our needs can actually cause us to take less responsibility for our own health and well-being. What is worse, living through our own needs to excess can lead to conflict and broken relationships through the emotional drain it can have on them.

The good news, however, is that when we reach the point where we are ready to name and acknowledge feelings in the presence of God, and also to seek after a right spirit with which we feel them, we open ourselves to the power of God to heal personal and relational brokenness. One of the ways this happens is through the power of forgiveness, to which we now turn our attention.

6

Forgiveness

As important as feeling our feelings is, it can be risky business. There is always the possibility that we will get bogged down in nursing hurt and anger and resentment. I have underscored the fact that identifying, acknowledging, and constructively expressing these feelings is essential to living with serenity and courage. Negative feelings that lurk in the shadows have power to determine attitudes and actions. They make our day. We cannot hide from them and at the same time expect to be unaffected by them.

Ultimately, however, negative feelings have to be let go. Once identified and expressed, we have to give them up or they will begin to dominate us. Holding on to negative feelings may be the most common reason why we have so much trouble letting go of situations over which we have no control, and don't have energy to do something about those things we can do something about. Feeling feelings is important to our mental and spiritual health, but in itself it is not enough to move us ahead. On the contrary, just the opposite is the case. Without taking the next step, feeling negative feelings can become counterproductive. That next step is giving them up.

Giving up negative feelings is an act of forgiveness. Forgiveness is essential to the process of inner healing. Being able to forgive is a reliable sign that we have given our will over to the power of God to work in and through us. No act of compassion, no deed of mercy, no amount of money donated to a good cause, no level of faithful attendance to religious ceremony or ritual compares to the act of forgiveness in affirming that we have learned to work the Serenity Prayer.

The importance of forgiveness is recognized by secular as well as religious writers. In her book *How to Make Love All the Time*, Barbara De Angelis concludes with a section on forgiveness. Her book is about relationships. She discusses at length what to do when a relationship has reached the point of being irretrievably broken. She says relationships that cannot be repaired must at least be healed to avoid carrying negative feelings into other relationships. Healing those relationships is for her an act of forgiveness. She writes:

> Healing a relationship with a former partner doesn't necessarily mean that you will be good friends afterwards—just that you have released and resolved the negative feelings and come to a place of understanding and forgiveness.[26]

One of the helpful distinctions she makes is between forgiveness and approval.[27] She points out that forgiveness does not mean we approve of what someone has said or done, only that we have grown to the point of understanding what motivated the person as well as recognizing anything we might have done to create or allow the incident to occur. That means we forgive ourselves and the other person. Forgiveness is not saying what happened was OK. It is a conscious act of putting what happened behind us.

In her popular book, *Return to Love,* Marianne Williamson writes: "Forgiveness is the key to inner peace because it is the mental technique by which our thoughts are transformed from fear to love....The places in our personality where we tend to deviate from love are not our faults, but our wounds."[28]

We may know this to be true. At some level most people know forgiveness is important, but most people also find it hard to do. In this failure we increase the difficulty we already have in accepting things that cannot be changed and changing things that can and should be. In many situations we do not lack the wisdom to know what to do. We lack the will to forgive and move ahead.

Saying we lack the will to forgive sounds like a hard word that ignores the hurt we have experienced. Yet it is said only to draw attention to an important point not to be missed. Forgiveness is another choice that we have to make in life. It is an act of the will, "a conscious decision to focus on love and let the rest go."[29] Facing things we cannot change is hard enough. When those situations require us to let go of some anger or injury, the difficulty increases significantly. It may well be that our capacity to accept things we cannot change in life is directly proportional to our willingness to forgive a wrong done to us. The tighter we cling to hurt the harder we bump our heads against those things beyond our control to change.

Refusing to forgive also makes it more difficult to focus on the things we can do something about in our lives. Nothing makes a person wallow in misery more and persist in playing the role of a victim than withholding forgiveness. It becomes like a poison that runs throughout the body, eventually making the whole person sick. Refusing to forgive wounds the spirit much more than any wrong another person might inflict on us.

On the other hand, forgiveness empowers us to let go of things we cannot change and move quickly to that which needs our attention. This is the case because it is the act of choosing to accept things that cannot be changed with serenity. Earlier I made the distinction between acceptance

and acceptance with serenity. Forgiveness—either of ourselves or another, or both—is the key. There is no room for
serenity in the life of anyone who nurses hurt.

An unforgiving spirit is a poison that will make us very
"sick." Its effect is always inwardly and outwardly destructive. However we might be trying to work the Serenity
Prayer, an unforgiving spirit will undercut our efforts. This
is one of those obvious, commonsense realities that we so
often overlook or choose to ignore. Until we are able to
forgive a wrong done to us, negative feelings will make us
unhappy, bitter, and eventually self-destructive. If we persist long enough in withholding forgiveness, the anger we
are nursing will most likely push us into severe depression.

The relationship between forgiveness and serenity and
courage is something we seem immediately to resist. Many
years ago a woman in a church I was serving whose family had been friends of mine got upset and said some rather
unkind things about me. She went out of her way to make
her feelings obvious to me and others. Not long thereafter
I left to go to another church. I remember that a year later
I found myself still thinking about what had happened in
my previous ministry, even getting angry as my thoughts
would focus on how unfair the woman had been and how
deeply she had hurt me. That continued for a long time. It
was not until I made the conscious choice to forgive her
that I realized withholding forgiveness was the reason I
could not find any peace about what had happened.

I knew I could not go back and change one thing about
the situation. Yet buffeted by a well-masked self-righteous-
ness that assured me that she had been wrong and unfair,
I held on to my hurt. Not until I forgave her was I able to
accept with serenity what had happened and my powerlessness to do anything about it. More important, though,
was the fact that it was not until then that I was able feel
like I was truly free of a bad experience that had happened a long time before.

This experience raises the issue of the relationship
between forgiving and forgetting. Often we hear someone
say, "I can forgive, but I cannot forget." While that makes

sense on a feeling level, it would seem that experience suggests there is very little forgiving without forgetting. I would submit that truer to experience is that forgiveness and forgetting must go together. They are inseparable. Someone has said that forgiving but not forgetting is like burying the hatchet while leaving the handle sticking up out of the ground. Forgetting a hurt we have experienced or a wrong done to us or an injustice we have suffered is central to letting go of what has happened. Forgiving but not forgetting is self-destructive because it allows external circumstances to have control over us. A past hurt will always hold on to us as long as we hold on to it.

Forgetting is, of course, a very difficult thing to do. Part of the trouble, however, may be in how we understand what it means to forget. It is what can be called "selective remembering."[30] It is an act of turning our will and our lives over to the care of God who empowers us to get some emotional distance from the person so that what happened to cause the hurt or pain or anger does not enter our conscious mind at the least provocation. The injury is no longer a primary focus. With the passage of time it recedes more and more out of the picture.

It is probably the case that the relationship between forgiving and forgetting hinges less on its possibleness than upon how willing we are to allow God's power to work in us. Again, the issue is not one of giving approval to what happened, or even to suggest that relationships have not been permanently altered. Sometimes they have been. It is simply to say that forgiveness involves a conscious openness to being empowered by God to let go of the past.

The following statement describes specifically what forgetting a past hurt or injury means:

> When a person forgives another, he [she] is promising to do three things about the intended wrongdoing; not to use it against the wrongdoer in the future; not to talk about it to others; not to dwell on it himself [herself].[31]

These three steps offer practical advice that works. The key, as in everything we have said, is our own attitude. It is the one inescapable factor for working the Serenity Prayer.

What needs to be underscored is the relationship between forgiveness and accepting what cannot be changed and changing what can and ought to be changed. Forgiveness speaks of hope in the worst of circumstances that lifts us above the temptation to become embittered and cynical. Forgiveness is a concrete act that demonstrates our readiness to accept responsibility for ourselves, our happiness, our quality of life. Forgiving another is the best decision we can ever make for ourselves. Its consequence is a healthy spirit.

Forgiveness is so important to working the Serenity Prayer because it reveals without equivocation whether or not we want to draw upon the power of God in specific situations. We like to think of ourselves as forgiving people. It is in specific situations, however, that we find out for sure. I considered myself a forgiving person who bore no grudges until I faced the fact that I had never forgiven the woman in my first church who hurt me deeply.

Serenity to accept things we cannot change and courage to change things needing changing depend upon the power of God. It is not in us to do either with any measure of effectiveness or consistency. But the power of God cannot abide where an unforgiving spirit dominates. The Lord's Prayer says, "Forgive us our sins, as we forgive those who sin against us." That implies that we cannot be forgiven unless we forgive. That is a hard word. Perhaps its deeper meaning lies in the fact that experiencing God's forgiveness depends upon our forgiving others. In other words, withholding forgiveness hardens our own hearts so that we are unable to accept forgiveness for ourselves.

Experiencing forgiveness is very humbling. It forces us to face up to our own sin and failures. It makes us know just how human we are. But it is when we face our humanness, I am learning, that we truly find healing, comfort, and the strength to forgive others, to let go of past hurts. The relationship between accepting and giving forgiveness is very much like the relationship between giving and receiving love. One cannot exist without the other, which is what the Lord's Prayer seems to be saying.

It is also true that giving and receiving forgiveness frees us from bitterness so that we can openly grieve our hurts and pains from situations we want to change but cannot. As we think about things we wish we could change, it is likely that we feel a lot of hurt and pain for ourselves and those we care about who are in those situations. Experience suggests that the more we are able to let go of negative feelings, the more we are able to feel this hurt and pain. The paradox of healing is that the more we feel the hurt and pain of life, the deeper we are able to enter into inward peace and serenity—moreover, the more perceptive and receptive we become to situations in which change is possible.

In my special group are people who are working at forgiving others who have done great injury to them. Every day they forgive and forget in order not to become so embittered by situations beyond their control that they cannot let them go. Together we remind one another that when we are tempted to hold on to a past hurt, as we often are, we shall never really know serenity, or even have the common sense to distinguish between things we can and cannot change, unless we have a forgiving spirit. We sometimes resist this kind of reminder. But continuing to participate in the group eventually leads us to acknowledge that at the center of this resistance is pride.

Pride is at the heart of our resistance to accepting things we cannot change, and makes serenity impossible even if we take the step toward acceptance. The reason is clear enough from what has already been said. Pride pushes out God. It precludes accepting God's will and help in carrying it out. Pride makes feelings more important than healing. Thus we cling to negative feelings instead of finally letting them go. What complicates the situation is that pride protects itself. Pride keeps us from admitting that pride is why we won't let go of a past hurt or injury. Pride keeps us from admitting that pride is dominating us.

Forgiving others for something they have done to us, to someone we love—and even to themselves—requires a decision to put the wisdom of God above our own. When we decide God's will is more important than our own, then we humble ourselves enough to begin searching to know the divine will in whatever circumstances we face. It is at that point that we have a real chance to accept with serenity what we cannot change and find the courage to change what can and should be changed.

Forgiving another is an act of respect. To forgive reveals a basic attitude of respect for others, that we see them as people worthy of being treated with dignity. The refusal to forgive is the refusal to acknowledge another, the refusal to recognize them as a person. Withholding forgiveness is dehumanizing. In this sense it is an act of violence. It turns a person into an object to be accepted or rejected at will. Nothing is more destructive than the refusal to forgive. It wounds all those involved.

One of the ways we gain strength to forgive is to recognize our own need for it. It is impossible to live in relationships with others and not need forgiving. All of us hurt each other. Acknowledging the ways we have hurt others, and even going so far as to ask them to forgive us, encourages us to forgive those who have hurt us. What we receive we are then able to give. The will to forgive plays a significant role in any serious attempt to work the Serenity Prayer. Indeed, the person who is unwilling to become a forgiving person is someone who will never know how to live inside out. Serenity has not substance apart from forgiveness; courage has no integrity. The wisest decision we can make in hurtful situations is to seek forgiveness and to give it. Healing is not possible without.

None of what has been said should overshadow the fact that forgiving others is a *process*. That is to say, it often does not happen quickly even when we choose to do it. Our humanness means the act of forgiving is part of the process of growing, and growth is not instantaneous. What is important is the decision to work at forgiving. That decision means it will happen, if we do not abandon our commitment to learning how to live inside out.

7

Dancing

ead the following story:

"Last week, from a distance, I saw an attractive young woman dancing. Her steps were graceful and energetic as she kept time with the music.

When we were introduced, Esther hesitated briefly before greeting me with her broad smile. Conversation with her was smooth and comfortable.

Beneath her black hair, her eyes sparkled dark and beautiful, commanding her gaze. Her face and arms were covered with scars from a severe burn, her skin gnarled and pulled from what must have been a long difficult healing process. Yet everything about her reflected confidence.

Later she danced again. I stood next to one of the religious leaders of the group…and remarked, "She sure dances well."

This man's observation was brief, but deep in what he was teaching me. He said, "She has much spiritual energy."

I like the way he phrased that. It invited my wonder about what tragedy had struck in Esther's life, what struggles she had gone through, what lessons she had drawn that would give her so much "spiritual energy."[32]

Esther's story speaks of healing, about experiencing a trauma that must have felt like reaching the end of the rope, and then learning how to live again, learning how to "dance" again. That is what inner healing is. That is what letting go ultimately feels like—dancing! "Dancing" symbolizes learning to live in spite of the circumstances that we may face. It is about what happens when we choose to accept the reality of choice in life.

The image of dancing is alive. It implies that we play a significant role in our own healing. And we do. Reaching the end of the rope and then letting go places us in the position of taking responsibility for making our lives into a dance. A friend once described his experience of having a nervous breakdown when he was a young man in his twenties. He said the psychiatrist with whom he worked was just the person he needed. After several conversations, my friend said the doctor candidly told him: "You can wallow in your problems, wasting away a life that others would like to have a chance to live, or you can pull yourself together and get on with living." The choice was his, and he chose living.

The telling of this story is not meant to suggest that what the doctor told this friend would be the appropriate response to everyone in a similar situation. But the choice to live—to dance—to heal—is one each of us must make every day as we face situations that need to be accepted or changed. And without realizing it, many of us are wasting away lives that others would like to have the chance to live. That is not said to make one feel guilty, but only to underscore the tragedy of so many people refusing to learn how to "dance" again.

My cousin's twenty-three-year-old son was killed in an automobile accident eight years ago. We were talking about him, and I asked her how she had been able to handle his death. She replied, "Well, the first thing you have to do is to decide *if* you're going to handle it."

She spoke the kind of wisdom that you sense immediately speaks to the deepest truths about life when you hear it. It really is true that life is a terrible thing to waste. Most of us think life is forever, that we have all the time we want to do what we want. It is an illusion. More to reality is the fact that life is very short, and the longer one lives, the shorter it becomes. Years pass so quickly.

It was only yesterday when we graduated from college, when our first child was born, when we got our first "real" job, when we lost our parents. Now when we look into the mirror we see the years are showing. There are still so many things to do, but we're afraid we don't have enough time to do them. We may believe in the eternalness of life, yet when we look into the future what we see is an end to what we wish would never end.

Obviously the length of life is something over which we have only a measure of control. But all of us can determine the quality of each day we do have. We can decide that we are going to "handle" whatever comes to us. That is what the Serenity Prayer says to me. The moment we open our eyes in the morning we have a choice to make about it. The quality of that moment, that hour, that day depends less on what is going on outside us than what is going on inside. We can choose to let external circumstances set the agenda, or we can choose to live inside out:

> Henceforth, each morning I will awake and fall on my knees and give thanks to God for the gift that only He can bestow—a new day. This is my most priceless possession. If I should ever feel ungrateful and treat this miracle lightly, I need only open my morning newspaper to the obituary page and

scan the list of names there—names of people who would be most pleased to change places with me despite my problems. There are no problems in a cemetery. I would rather be here than there. I am grateful for this opportunity.[33]

That is so obvious, isn't it? Yet the obvious things in life are often the most difficult to learn. Once, the great Scottish-born preacher, Peter Marshall, was asked what passages in the Bible he didn't understand. He replied that he did not worry much about the ones he didn't understand because he had enough trouble with the ones he did. That is the way living life is for most of us. The obvious things give us the most trouble.

There are no exceptions from tough times for anyone. Some people seem to have more than their share, though. We do not understand that. What we can understand, however, is that whether the burden is heavy or light, we have a say in how well we live. We determine to a significant extent whether we dance or give in to despair. Which one it is depends on how much we want to dance. How much do we want to live? The Serenity Prayer puts this challenge before us. It assumes that life is not easy. It assumes that we will have days when we feel overwhelmed by troubles. It assumes we will have to make things happen if we don't want to end up sitting around wondering what happened. Praying the Prayer is a practical way to say we want to have a big say in how well we live.

This is the point I said at the beginning that Scott Peck makes in *The Road Less Traveled*. Life is difficult, not for some people, but for everyone. Healthy living is a matter of what we do with the difficulties. We can moan about problems or solve them. Meeting and solving problems, Peck says, is what gives life meaning:

Problems are the cutting edge that distinguishes between success and failure. Problems call forth our courage and wisdom; indeed, they create our courage and wisdom. It is only because of problems that we grow mentally and spiritually.[34]

So important is solving problems to the health of the human spirit that Peck is convinced, as a practicing psychiatrist, that avoiding problems is the primary basis of all human mental illness.

The Bible has something to say about the role we play in our own healing. Once Jesus met a man in Jerusalem by the Sheep Gate pool who had been ill for thirty-eight years. Tradition had it that an angel would trouble the waters of the pool from time to time, and those who managed to get in at that moment would be healed. According to the story, when Jesus saw the man, and knowing full well he had been coming there for thirty-eight years, he asked the startling question, "Do you want to be healed?" It seems reasonable to conclude that for this man healing was dependent upon how much he really wanted it. Was the fact that he had been coming so long without results an indication that he had grown accustomed to letting things happen to him? Was the reason he gave that he had no one to help him get in the pool the words of a man who thought of himself as a victim of life's injustice? Did the question suggest that healing has as much to do with the spirit as the body?

Whatever else this question, "Do you want to be healed?" may have meant, at the very least it challenges any notion that we are helpless in the face of difficult circumstances. Life is not always what we make of it, but we always have to make something of it, if we are going to have anything. Moreover, that has to be done in the midst of the ups and downs that come to us all. There are no excuses for not getting into the water.

That is the way life is, isn't it? Nothing much happens until we step into the water. In other words, nothing happens until we start making it happen, until, shall we say, we start dancing. The Serenity Prayer gives us a way to do that. Its wisdom is that the principles it embodies apply to the whole of life, to problems big and small, to good days and bad ones, to the thrill of victory and the agony of defeat. The Prayer's challenge encompasses all of life. We may not feel like dancing, but we can anyway, if we truly want to.

How do we make the choice to live again? How does one face the trauma of severe burns, as Esther did, and then have the will to dance again? The answer lies in what we have already said—when we accept the fact that we have a choice to dance or not to dance. That is the critical factor—facing the choice before us. But when we do, we make a great discovery: healing—dancing—does not depend upon our own strength alone. The power of one beyond us, a higher power, if you will, gives us the strength to dance. All we have to do is to start where we are with what we've got to start with.

The Catholic sister, Mother Teresa of Calcutta, is known all over the world for her work with the poorest of the poor in India. In 1985 she was awarded the Noble Peace Prize for her work. She can be described as a person who made the decision to "dance" in the midst of terrible suffering all around her. She says that when she and the other sisters first began their work they had nothing with which to help the poor. But God, she says, "took our nothing and made it into something."[35]

Working the Serenity Prayer is like asking God to take what feels like the "nothing" in our lives and make it something. That is what "dancing" life means. The Serenity Prayer helps us to dance. On the surface this may seem too much to ask, especially if we feel like we have reached the end of our rope. Yet how can we experience the power God gives us to live well in all situations, except to act even if we feel like doing anything is more than we can handle? People who want to accept with serenity things they cannot change bad enough, and want the courage to change things that should be changed bad enough, and have some clearness about both, do what they have to do, only to discover that they did what they did in a given situation precisely at the time they did not believe they could do anything.

At the same time, we want to be careful not to suggest that the life of someone who prays the Serenity Prayer will become a "success" story about the power of prayer, or that everything will always turn out well for them. That certainly has not been my experience. In fact, prayer "success" stories can be very troubling. Yesterday I was turning the dial on my car radio to find a clear station when I came upon an announcer on a Christian radio station praying for people who had sent in prayer requests. Several times she reported "success" stories of people whose lives had turned out just right. While we do not want to question the sincerity of this woman, or those who give testimonies to answered prayer, it seems that more often than not an answer to prayer does not mean there is a change in an external situation. More true to reality is that there is a change in the way we cope with it.

The Serenity Prayer is the one prayer that forces anyone who is serious about being happy to accept personal responsibility for it. It is a kind of "tough love" prayer. Its wisdom lies in the balance between trusting the power of God and doing our part to help ourselves. The Serenity Prayer works only when we recognize that it is hard work. It is work because there are decisions to be made and things to be done. It is hard because we are prone to giving up on living a meaning-full life when it involves work. Here again, Scott Peck is helpful when he discusses at length the natural resistance we humans have to spiritual/emotional healthiness, using physical evolution as a point of analogy. He notes that the most striking feature of the process of physical evolution is that it is a miracle:

> Given what we understand of the universe, evolution should not occur; the phenomenon should not exist. One of the basic natural laws is the second law of thermodynamics, which states that energy naturally flows from a state of greater organization to a state of lesser organization...in other words, the universe is in the process of winding down....Ultimately...in billions and billions of years, the universe will completely wind down until it reaches the lowest point as an amorphous, totally disorganized, totally undifferentiated "blob" in which nothing happens any more. This state of

total disorganization and undifferentiation is termed entropy.[36]

This "flow" of entropy is against the "flow" of evolution because evolution is the process of development from lower to higher and higher states of complexity, differentiation, and organization. Humans are at the top of this process, yet the natural flow of energy, i.e., the flow of entropy, is in the opposite direction. As Peck says, in the ordinary course of things, we humans should not even exist.

From this discussion of physical evolution, Peck moves to the realm of the spiritual. He suggests that the spiritual evolution of human beings is similar to the physical, making the point that spiritual growth does not come naturally or easily:

> ...the process of spiritual growth is an effortful and difficult one. This is because it is conducted against a natural resistance, against a natural inclination to keep things the way they were, to cling to the old maps and old ways of doing things, to take the easy path.[37]

Experience suggests that Peck is correct in his assessment of the resistance people have to sustained spiritual growth and development that leads to meaningful living. The Serenity Prayer takes this resistance seriously. It is a prayer of hope because it trusts in a God who serves as the force and power in us to help us grow and develop spiritually. At the same time, it is grounded in the reality that God helps us grow; God does not "make" us grow. We have an indispensible role to play in our own serenity making. The truth of the Serenity Prayer is experienced only by those who work it. It is just that simple, and just that difficult. Learning to dance again requires energy and discipline to overcome the natural inclinations we have to give up, to stay where we are, and then to complain about it. But we can dance again. That is the good news. Others have learned how. We can, too.

8

Freedom

To learn to dance, for the first time or all over again, means making the decision to put ourselves in the position of finally being free. This is no ordinary freedom we have been talking about. It is freedom of a special character because it is rooted in serenity, courage, and wisdom. It is the kind of freedom that creates a fundamental shift in the way we live. It even frees us from the anxiety that we might lose it. To live in fear that we might lose our freedom is not to be free. Freedom and the fear of losing it co-exist only when freedom is external. Inward freedom has no fear. That is the secret of its power. It is the kind of freedom that accepts each day as an expression of divine grace, and responds in gratitude and joy for having been given that one day. Living one day at a time means celebrating life from the center of one's inner freedom.

The Serenity Prayer is a road to this kind of freedom because it is a process of learning how to let go. That is the simple truth of the Prayer, which is at the same time easy to understand and difficult to trust. The Serenity Prayer presents a clear challenge. We can choose to let go of the illusion of external control and learn to live from the inside out, or we can choose not to let go. Which choice we make will determine the quality of our living. The responsibility for that choice rests squarely on our shoulders. Life may be difficult, but trouble does not take away our freedom, unless we choose to allow that to happen. People who know how to live inside out are free people who know no fear of losing their freedom. They know what freedom with serenity is. They have gained the wisdom to refuse both to worry about tomorrow and to look back to yesterday. They are free to live as they best know how, and refuse to give up their freedom to anyone else's expectations of them.

There is no greater freedom than to be free from living by other people's expectations. The person who truly prays the Serenity Prayer, who lives it, has chosen to be set free from this kind of self-imposed tyranny. Inner freedom resists tyranny of every kind, and is always successful in doing so. That is the miracle of it. It is the most powerful force in the world. What is more, it is readily available to anyone. The only people who do not have this kind of freedom are those who choose not to.

The freedom found through the Serenity Prayer is the kind the Apostle Paul refers to in his Letter to the Galatians: "For freedom Christ has set us free. Stand firm, therefore, and do not submit again to a yoke of slavery" (Galatians 5:1). Here the Apostle is speaking confessionally. It is not that Paul is encouraging rejection of the Torah law that he had been schooled in as a faithful Jew. Rather, he is pointing to a kind of freedom he has found that transcends the law, a freedom that can only be described as inward freedom, freedom that is not subject to external circumstances, laws, customs, or expectations. Experiencing this kind of freedom is what led him to confess:

> ...for I have learned to be content with whatever I
> have. I know what it is to have little, and I know

what it is to have plenty. In any and all circumstances I have learned the secret of being well-fed
and of going hungry, of having plenty and of being
in need.

Philippians 4:11b–12

Other translations of verse 11 say, "I have learned in whatever state I am, to be content" (RSV).

The point is that the Apostle had discovered an inner
freedom that had made him realize that the quality of his
living did not depend upon external circumstances. He had
the kind of freedom no one could take away from him. The
only way he could lose it would be to choose to give it up.

That is the kind of freedom the Serenity Prayer leads
to because it is freedom that is a gift of God. The problem
we humans have in trying to gain our freedom is that we
act on the unchallenged assumption that it is something
we gain on our own. The Serenity Prayer does not say
that. In fact, it says just the opposite. Praying the Serenity Prayer is itself an acknowledgment that we do not have
the capacity to give ourselves the kind of freedom we desire. Instead, it positions us to receive freedom as a gift, a
by-product, so to speak, of that positioning. In choosing to
give up the illusion of external control, we position ourselves to discover the inward gift of unconditional freedom God put inside us at the beginning of creation.

This is what Adam and Eve lost for all of us. In their
quest for autonomy, they enslaved themselves—and the
whole of humanity—to the illusion that freedom was external—being free to do whatever we want to do. Rather
than becoming free, they yoked themselves to the worst
kind of tyranny—the illusion of control that leads to bondage masked as freedom. One might even say that it was
only after humanity had lived long enough under the law
that was made necessary because of the abuse of external
freedom that inner freedom was even possible. The illusion of control had to be exposed before we would choose
genuine freedom. That is what the Apostle Paul was trying to help the Galatians understand.

The inner freedom to which the Serenity Prayer leads rests, of course, upon the reality of human limitations. Were we able to control external circumstances, we might be able to create freedom without anxiety. But that is not possible. Being human means living with limitations. Freedom, therefore, is always conditional when it is external. The only unconditional, absolute freedom that exists is inward, and that is rooted in the recognition that God is God, and we must give up yesterday and tomorrow to God, and live in the moment. That is a gift that in all candor we have to confess we do not deserve. Not to be chained to yesterday or frightened by tomorrow is almost too good to be true. But people who live by the Serenity Prayer have learned that it is true, indeed.

Living inside out means being the persons we were created to be. When we are at home within ourselves, we have the spiritual balance to be. This does not mean we are complacent about personal growth. We are always in the process of becoming. What inner freedom teaches us is that engaging in the process of becoming is what being the person we were created to be means. As long as our capacity to live fully is dependent upon external circumstances, we are not able to live as children of God. Thus, we are not able to grow into deeper spiritual maturity. It is our nature to be inwardly free. Living as people of God means living from the inside out. Whenever we choose to surrender our inner freedom, we are choosing to give up the very nature of who we are. It is, as we have said throughout, a choice we face daily.

Part of who we are is being a blessing to each other. The freer we are inwardly, the more we become a blessing to the lives of those around us. Being a blessing to others is a measure of what it means to be human. God called Abraham to be a blessing to all the nations (Genesis 12:3). As Abraham's seed, the call to bless others includes all who believe in God. This happens in several ways.

One way is to be free enough not to try to possess others. In his book *Fire in the Belly*, Sam Keen describes his own painful experience of learning how to love someone without trying to possess that person. He was in a love relationship that he wanted very much, but it was not working. He had tried to hold on in every way he knew. Finally he reached a point of inner freedom when he was able to let go, and at the same time continue to love this woman he wanted so much. His description of that moment is poignant:

> I found a phone booth and called her. For the first time in weeks she answered. "I know it is time for you to go," I said. "As much as I want to be with you, I know there is no way for us to remain lovers. I am too old and too raw to be casual about love and you are too young to be faithful and make graceful commitments. Go, without deception or guilt. I love you. Good-bye.[38]

At that moment he became a blessing in her life. He could love without possessing. Though painful, to be sure, it is the only way to live that is truly freeing. It doesn't happen quickly, but this kind of freedom is the reliable fruit of praying the Serenity Prayer.

Inner freedom also leads us to resist being possessed. My personal experience in working the Serenity Prayer is that at a point, almost unexpected, I knew that I had gained sufficient emotional independence from those I love to live my own life without being controlled by the tyranny of what I thought they expected of me. That was a significant moment in my life. It was when I knew that I was truly free.

Living without letting others possess us blesses others because it confronts them with the challenge to become free themselves. Men and women are conditioned by culture and tradition to be "owned" through the emotional hold the roles they have been assigned have on them. Claiming our freedom from this form of tyranny is no easy task. It may be that awareness of what has been done to us can lead us to make this claim, but it is just as likely that awareness alone is not enough. A power greater than knowledge that propels us toward inner freedom is needed.

The Serenity Prayer connects us to such a power—God. In God we find the strength and power to live and love without allowing anyone to possess us. That is to be free to bless others.

The freedom to live without possessing and without being possessed leads to another way we bless the lives of others. We are free to be truly present to them. A colleague of mine has been known for his pastoral presence to students, former students, and area ministers for many years. He is a blessing in the lives of so many people. He was once described as someone who is "at home inside himself." It was not only an accurate description, but a very telling one. The power of his pastoral presence is rooted in his inner freedom to be himself all the time. Yet he would be the first to say that his inner freedom has not come easy. He is at home enough with himself to acknowledge his own need for acceptance. Yet daily he chooses to live inside out, which provides him with the strength of presence to be a pastor to others. That is what living with serenity really means.

The irony, of course, in talking about being a blessing in the lives of others is that more often than not we receive a blessing ourselves. It may even be the case that the quality of our personal spiritual maturity is proportional to the extent to which we bless the lives of others. Here, again, the fact that serenity is the gift of God is never more apparent. How many times have we had the experience of helping someone else and in doing so finding that it helped us put things in our own lives in perspective.

A woman known for her work among the poor and marginalized in our city was experiencing a crisis with her sister that was disrupting her personal and family life. She found herself weary from trying to control the situation. She started praying for the serenity to give up her need for control, and courage to do what she gained the wisdom to know she could and should do. She finally began to let go. As she did she said she felt renewed energy to get back into her ministry to others, which turned into a blessing for herself as she experienced a renewed sense of worth and joy. That is the effect inner freedom has in our lives. We bless and are blessed by others.

Inner freedom. Nothing is comparable to its contagious joy or its redemptive power. In the final analysis it is the freedom to live and to die. It is the freedom to define ourselves, to assert our "being" above our "doing." It is the fruit of the paradox of divine grace that gives us control of our lives as we relinquish control to God. That is, in the end, the essence of what it means to pray the Serenity Prayer and to learn how to live inside out.

> God give us grace to accept with serenity things
>   that cannot be changed;
> courage to change things that should be changed;
> and wisdom to distinguish the one from the other.
>
> Living one day at a time;
> enjoying one moment at a time;
> accepting hardships as the pathway to peace.
> Taking, as He did, this sinful world as it is, not as
>   I would have it.
> Trusting that He will make all things right if
>   I surrender to His will.
> That I may be reasonably happy in this life
> and supremely happy with Him forever in the next.
> Amen.

Epilogue

On several occasions throughout this discussion reference has been made to the important role a small group of people have played—and continue to play—in my personal experience of learning how to pray the Prayer and work its power into my life. Words fall very short of expressing what these people mean to me. But what may be able to be conveyed is the fact that working the Serenity Prayer is not something to be done alone. A small group provides the context in which support and candid discussion together make personal growth richer and deeper—and even inevitable.

These kinds of small groups exist in abundance in almost every community. What has been personally disappointing to me, however, is the fact that I had to go outside the church to find such a group. Churches have for many years experimented with small group life. Some have actually stayed with them and streamlined them into the core of their congregational life. Most, though, have floundered and dissolved. Others tend to become focused on social issues and community ministries, none of which is bad, but in the long run tends to take the group's focus away from nurturing members in learning how to live inside out.

Twelve Step programs of various kinds are the fastest-growing groups in the United States today. A comment often heard from those who participate is that they had never experienced the depth of spiritual development they have found in these groups in the church. Many of them believe they had to go outside the church to experience the reality of God's presence and power for themselves. A lot of them continue to attend church, but their source of spiritual help comes from their Twelve Step group.

Some of us in the church might be tempted to argue with this perception of church life, and also of the value of Twelve Step programs. But for most people perception is reality, and the perception is that help in genuine spiritual growth has to be found outside the church. Worship services, fellowship groups, study classes may be important opportunities for them. Yet nothing the church offers seems to give them what they find in groups outside the church.

Were we, however, to accept this perception as accurate, identifying why it is remains problematic. Group dynamics are complex. Why one group works and another one doesn't has no simple answer. Just as enigmatic is why some groups seem to depend upon the personalities of certain people, while the quality of the experience in another group seems to transcend personalities. I think, however, that there is one primary reason Twelve Step programs work the way they do for people. It is the principle of anonymity. It is believed to be the spiritual foundation for the group's life. Anonymity is why people dare to come to Twelve Step groups. Without it the risk of exposure and embarrassment is too great.

Anonymity is a problem in the church. The nature of congregational life flies in the face of it. Congregations are part of an extended community in which a particular church is located. Even in the kind of impersonal urban and suburban communities most people live in, we are known, if not through neighborhood connections, then through work and community organizations and service. Anonymity is simply not an option in the church's life, and perhaps on theological grounds, not even desirable. In Christ we are called to be with each other, to know each other, to live and serve and die with each other. Anonymity simply does not fit into this way of thinking. The church is supposed to be that place where we can be known—just as we are.

Even without anonymity, though, I believe it is possible to form small groups in the church that help people learn how to turn their lives and their wills over to God. Confidentiality, rather than anonymity, is possible in the church, and with the passage of time can function to encourage freedom of sharing in the way that anonymity does.

I want to suggest that the Serenity Prayer can serve as an effective initial focal point for such a group. Should other materials become the focus later, the Serenity Prayer can remain a defining anchor for the group's life. Let me identify some principles that enhance the possibility that this kind of group(s) will succeed.

First, the group's single purpose needs to be stated clearly—to learn how to pray the Serenity Prayer, that is, to work it. It must be made clear that the forming group is not a study group. The group's purpose is to effect change in people's lives by the members helping one another learn how to live inside out. Study groups are for study. What personal impact the study has on the members is secondary. A Serenity Prayer group is not interested simply in people "studying" the Prayer. The group exists to position people to allow the Prayer to change their lives.

Because of the nature of the group, it is important to make the purpose clear to insure that people understand the purpose is not negotiable. Sometimes people want to be in a small group, but for reasons other than the stated purpose. The one who calls the Serenity Prayer group together has to be strong enough to resist this kind of pressure. Further, any use of the questions and exercises that begin on page 104 should be within the context of the stated purpose of the group.

A second principle that can help the group form is to keep the size small. Five to ten people is ideal. Further, the more groups that are formed, the more flexibility there will be for people to attend. Multiple groups can meet at different times and days, offering people the chance to attend another group's meeting when they are unable to attend their home group.

A third principle is that the meeting should last for an hour. There needs to be an opening and closing. Schedules today are such that people need to know the extent of their commitment when they join a group. The leader of the meeting should watch the time to make sure the hour's length is faithfully followed.

A fourth principle is that the focus of the group's discussion must be on the personal experiences of those attending in regard to praying the Serenity Prayer. Twelve step groups call this keeping the focus on ourselves. This is not a kind of selfish self-absorption, but an acceptance of one of the things the Serenity Prayer says—the only person we can change is ourselves. Since the group's purpose is personal growth and development through learning how to live the Serenity Prayer, it is only natural that the discussion would focus on how the participants are doing in this process.

An important part of keeping the focus on each one's personal experiences is trusting that the Holy Spirit will guide the group's life. This is a group that is trying to come to know God personally. Our faith affirms that God meets us in this desire. That is the work of the Holy Spirit this process trusts.

Keeping this kind of focus is also why any participant who has been in the group long enough to understand the group's purpose can lead one of the meetings. It is important that leadership be shared. Someone may be asked to be the group coordinator to take care of logistical details. Leading the meetings, however, can be shared precisely because everyone is a leader at the point of his or her personal experiences. The discussion simply needs to be initiated, not guided. There is no agenda in the group's meeting beyond the stated purpose. The leader trusts that the Spirit will work as the Spirit works, and that people will hear what they need to hear.

Implicit in what we are saying, of course, is the fact that "business" should be kept at a minimum in the meetings. There will be business. Groups don't meet for long without having to make some decisions. It is important that no discussion of business be extended beyond five minutes. It may be that someone is attending who desperately needs to hear what others have to say, or perhaps needs to talk about what is happening in their lives. Business cannot be allowed to rob anyone of this opportunity.

As we have noted, though anonymity is not constitutive to the group's life, confidentiality is. Every participant can hold sacred the trust all give to each that, in the words of Twelve Step groups, "What is said here, when you leave here, let it stay here." Any breaking of confidentiality that might occur must be dealt with openly and caringly. The group's life will be diminished if those who attend cannot trust everyone to keep confidences.

With these principles in mind, the following questions and exercises are offered to help individual readers work the Prayer. Both the questions and the exercises are intended to assist persons in the group in confronting the issues raised in the book on a personal level. The group leader may ask participants to share what they have learned from working at the questions and exercises, but the learnings should not become issues for debate. Different people will learn different things precisely because they are different. At the same time there will be enough commonality of experience for all the group participants to relate to what any member shares. This kind of sharing should help create a sense of a safe environment in which participants will be encouraged to become more and more open about what they are experiencing as they work the Serenity Prayer.

Introduction

1. Scott Peck says that "life is difficult." Write down several specific experiences you have had when life has been difficult.

2. Now try to remember the specific attitude you had during those experiences. Write these attitudes beside each experience.

3. How did the particular attitude you had help or hinder your ability to cope with these difficult situations?

4. Based upon what you have written, what kind of attitude most dominates the way you deal with problems?

5. Now read the Serenity Prayer several times. Stop and listen to each part of the first section and then ask yourself if the three parts of the Prayer describe the way you responded to the difficult experiences you wrote down. To help in this process, write the words *held on* or *let go* beside each experience to indicate when you tried to control the situation and when you trusted it to the care and wisdom of God.

6. Your responses to these exercises should give you a sense of where you are in knowing how to "pray" the Serenity Prayer. The questions and exercises for each chapter that follow are intended to help you go deeper into the meaning the Prayer can have in your life.

Chapter 1

1. Take time to write the story of your own spiritual journey. What is the most prominent image of God in what you have written? Does this picture of God help or hinder your personal relationship with God?

2. What does unconditional love mean to you? Do you remember being loved unconditionally by someone when you were a child? Did your church teach you that God loves you unconditionally?

3. Does the father's unconditional love in the parable of the prodigal son describe the way you now experience God?

4. Would you describe your relationship with God as one in which you believe in God or trust God? Describe a recent situation in which you have experienced this difference between believing in and trusting God.

Chapter 2

1. Would you describe yourself as someone who, on a consistent basis, is able to accept with serenity things, persons, and circumstances you cannot change?

2. Is there any situation at this moment that is troubling you? Is there anything about this problem you cannot change? Examine conversations you have had about this situation to see if your own words show that you have not really accepted the fact that you cannot control what is happening.

3. Did you live today as if the quality of your life was a matter of your choice? Write down the ways in which you made the choice to make the best of the day you were given.

4. Write down the expectations you have in the relationships that mean the most to you. Have you experienced in these relationships the fact that the level of your serenity is inversely proportional to the level of your expectations?

5. Count the number of times in the last month you have acted like a "people pleaser." Examine why you acted this way. Relive those situations and imagine how you could have acted that would not have been "people-pleasing."

6. Count the number of times in the last month you have acted like a "fixer." Examine why you acted this way. Relive those situations and imagine how you could have acted that would not have been "fixing."

7. Are you trying to control some problems you are facing by holding on to them? Can you trust God enough to accept what you cannot change about them?

Chapter 3

1. Write down ways in which you can change your life that will bring you more serenity.

2. Can you name instances when you have fallen into the role of playing a "victim"? Examine why you acted this way, and then imagine how you could have acted in a different way.

3. Are you a person who acts or simply reacts to other people? During the last week, have you acted or reacted in most of the difficult situations you have faced?

4. On a scale of 1 to 10, how committed are you to working on improving the quality of your life? One month from now ask yourself to what extent you have followed through on your commitment to self-improvement.

Chapter 4

1. Name the number of times recently that you have been a "fool" for more than five minutes a day.

2. Using your common sense, examine any situation that you are worrying about and identify very specifically what you can and cannot change about it. Note those instances where you are trying to change something beyond your control to change, and note those instances when you have or have not taken action when you could have changed the situation. Now ask yourself if you are you willing to change what you can change and to let go of what you cannot change.

3. As you think about how you respond to problems, do you have more trouble knowing what to do or doing what you already know is the wise thing to do?

4. Do you have someone who is a faithful friend? Are you using the gift they are in your life to keep yourself accountable for your own spiritual growth and development? If you do not have a faithful friend, pray for God to lead you to such a person, and then be alert for the signs that your prayer is being answered.

Chapter 5

1. Are you hesitant to express your true feelings to people? If so, examine why this is the case. Naming feelings is the first step in feeling them. Write down the feelings that are the most difficult for you to express.

2. Were you taught that there are "right" and "wrong" feelings? Offer all the feelings you have right now—positive or negative—to God in prayer. Try writing them down in a prayer. Can you trust that God accepts you just as you are, feelings and all? Until you can you will continue to be afraid to be honest about your feelings.

3. If you have been doing the exercises for each chapter, then you have already begun to experience the value of personal journaling. Keep at it! Its value will increase the more you use it. It will help you to know what kind of heart you really have.

4. Are you loving your spouse, children, or friends through your personal need for acceptance and approval? Work with how you feel about yourself. Do you love *you*? Remember that healthy love for others begins with yourself. And also remember that you are among the beloved of God just as you are.

Chapter 6

1. Name any negative feelings you are nursing and the person(s) at whom they are directed. Is nursing these feelings keeping you from healing from a past hurt, wound, or trauma?

2. Is nursing negative feelings your way of refusing to forgive the person who hurt you? Have you accepted the false notion that to forgive is like saying what happened was OK? When you have experienced being forgiven for something you did wrong, did you then think what happened was OK?

3. Are you trying to forgive without forgetting?

4. Write down the things you have done for which you needed to be forgiven. What does it feel like if the other person has not forgiven you?

5. How is your withholding forgiveness from someone affecting your prayer life? Does this person's face or name come to your mind when you pray for God to forgive you? Is that a sign that you are hurting yourself by not forgiving and not forgetting? Forgiving is hard to do. God never said it would be easy, only that it is possible.

Chapter 7

1. Describe what it would mean for you to begin to "dance" again in your life.

2. Name any circumstances you are facing in which you can choose to "dance" if you really want to. Do you believe you are wasting your life by not choosing to "dance"?

3. If "problems are the cutting edge that distinguishes between success and failure," as Scott Peck says, how do you assess the quality of your life up to now?

4. Identify the specific things you are doing that demonstrate that you are taking responsibility for your own growth toward spiritual healthiness.

Chapter 8

1. Write down what it would mean for you to be "content" in a troubling situation that you have faced or are facing now.

2. Has praying the Serenity Prayer in a specific situation helped you experience what you think the apostle Paul meant when he talked about being content in whatever state he found himself? If you have not yet worked the Prayer, are you willing to work it in the trust that you will experience this kind of contentment?

3. How many times this past week have your human limitations frustrated you?

4. Describe the situations you have faced when you experienced the inner freedom of giving up trying to possess someone or refusing to let them possess you.

5. Name the people who have been a blessing in your life. Now name the ways you have been a blessing in the lives of others.

6. Pray the Serenity Prayer again and again. Let its truth go deep in you. Each time you live it, you will know its truth, and you will be set free.

Notes

[1] M. Scott Peck, *The Road Less Traveled* (New York: Simon and Schuster, 1978), p. 15.

[2] Peck refers to the first of the "Four Noble Truths" Buddha taught—"Life is suffering." *(Ibid.)*

[3] From a New York Times News Service article that appeared in the *Lexington Herald Leader*, December 31, 1992.

[4] There are several versions of the first part of the Serenity Prayer. This particular version, focusing on serenity, courage, wisdom, comes from Ursula Niebuhr's *Remembering Reinhold Niebuhr* (San Francisco: Harper & Row, 1991). The lesser-known second half comes from the National AA office located in New York City.

[5] Carolyn Thomas, *Will the Real God Please Stand up* (New York: Paulist Press, 1991).

[6] Paul Tillich, "You Are Accepted," *The Shaking of the Foundations* (New York: Charles Scribner's Sons, 1948), p. 162.

[7] Pat Smith, "Inspiration Point," *Independence Express*, Independence, Missouri, January, 1990.

[8] This quote appears on the back of the jacket cover of the book, *Peace of Mind*, published by Simon & Schuster, 1946.

[9] Frederick Buechner, *Telling Secrets* (San Francisco: Harper, 1991), p. 27f.

[10]Jacqueline Syrup Bergan & S. Marie Schwan, *Birth: A Guide for Prayer* (Winona, Minnesota: Saint Mary's Press, 1985), p. 142.

[11]John Powell, SJ, *The Christian Vision* (Allen, Texas: Argus Communications, 1984), p. 7.

[12]From an article in *People Magazine*, November, 1990.

[13]William Glasser, *Reality Therapy: A New Approach to Psychiatry* (New York: Harper & Row, 1965).

[14]Theodore Roszak, *The Making of a Counter-Culture* (New York: Anchor Books, 1969).

[15]Robert Fulghum, *Everything I Really Need to Know I Learned in Kindergarten* (New York: Villard Books, 1988).

[16]Sue Monk Kidd, *When the Heart Waits* (San Francisco: Harper, 1990), p. 21.

[17]*Ibid.*, p. 22.

[18]*Ibid.*, p. 21.

[19]Elaine Prevallet, *Reflections on Simplicity* (Pendle Hill Pamphlet 244), p. 6.

[20]In the context of listening, she presupposes the need for inner quiet, a developed prayer life, and "the capacity to act of out something other than our heads." *(Ibid.)*

[21]This column originally appeared in *The Washington Post*.

[22]Sidney Jourard, *The Transparent Self* (Van Nostrand Reinhold, 1971), p. 6.

[23]Elton Trueblood, *The Encourager* (Nashville: Broadman Press, 1978).

[24]Rick Atkinson, *The Long Gray Line* (Boston: Houghton-Mifflin Co., 1989).

[25]*Ibid.*, p. 103.

[26]Barbara De Angelis, *How to Make Love All the Time* (New York: Dell Publishing, 1987), p. 261.

[27]*Ibid.*

[28]Marianne Williamson, *Return to Love* (HarperCollins, 1993), p. 81.

[29]*Ibid.*

[30]*Ibid.*

[31]A printed copy of this quote was given to me by a friend without any notation of authorship.

[32]A quote shared with me from a column by an Episcopal priest in a church paper unknown to me.

[33]Source unknown.

[34]Peck, p. 16.

[35]Mother Teresa made this statement to the press when she received the Nobel Peace Prize in December, 1979.

[36]Peck, p. 263f.

[37]*Ibid.*, p. 266.

[38]Sam Keen, *Fire in the Belly: On Being a Man* (New York: Bantam Books, 1991), p. 12.